ALL

Broken in *Spirit* Renewed in *Faith, Hope and Charity*

Mary Bird Young

Power Publishing, 2016

Published in the United States by Power Publishing 2016.
ISBN-13: 978-0692661895
ISBN-10: 0692661891

Kindle version available through Amazon.com (Purchasers of this print edition are eligible for discounted 'BookMatch' pricing for the Kindle edition for $2.99 USD)

Library of Congress Control Number (Pending)

Table of Contents

The purpose of this book is to increase proceeds to research on prevention and treatment of dementia and for Habitat for Humanity which is a worthy way to help people help themselves acquire good housing. Any profit gleaned from the sale of __ALL__ is pledged **to those charities. It is self-published on Amazon, CreateSpace.com, E books and Kindle through Bowker with Power Publishing Company.**

Preface

Under the cover of __ALL__ are two other writings: Mary Young's **Autobiographical Sketches. TED,** the story of her brother's life and his siege now with dementia. **Back from the Edge** is a continuation in How __ALL__ Came to Be.

The Autobiographical Sketches reveal the experiences in Mary's life that molded her faith. Much is written by and about Mary B. Young. It gives insight into why she would choose to write a book that blends science and religion as this one does. Others can be reminded of their own lives, through the narratives of her background. Their questioning and searching can lead them to a deeper spiritual life.

The uniqueness of __ALL__ is in its constant invitation to the readers to use their own creative thinking to address the problems in today's world and to join others in thinking of solutions for an abiding future for life on Earth. It combines religion and science by pointing to mankind's connection to the omniscient Mind and urges respect for and use of the scientific method of inquiry as a way of getting consistent results through repeat trials.

The views of the Central Oregon Cascades is a spiritual experience for many people. Gazing at them brings renewal. The cover picture of a smidge of Broken Top and the Three Sisters Mountains in the Cascade Range of Oregon was chosen by the writer to represent human spiritual growth. Search on line for more information and many pictures of this awesome range of mountains. Cascade Mountain Range – search Google

From South to North. There is Broken Top which erupted in the Pleistocene era creating an enormously high mountain. The extensive glacial erosion has left it a partial shield with a ruinous interior.

Broken Top erupted in the Pleistocene era and created an enormously high mountain. Extensive glacial, wind and water erosion left it open and ever more vulnerable to wounds. It seems to represent the brokenness of the human body and spirit from the painful episodes of life. For those who want to know more Google: The Cascade Mountain Range.

About The Author

Mary Bird Young is an observer and listener more than a believer by faith and she is certain that people everywhere do find a common God by different names, but ONE who is present with them, loves them and helps them help themselves through trials.

She has had among her closest friends, four Methodist ministers, a Lutheran Minister, two Episcopal Priests, a Catholic Priest, a Hindu, a Sikh, a Muslim, Jewish friends, and friends from every Christian faith. She has traveled to many countries and has exceptionally close friends from India, Pakistan, Australia, Mexico and Costa Rica. Many people from other countries have been guests in her home. She has been agnostic many times, but seldom atheistic. She does not understand the complete nature of God, but doubts that all that exists created itself.

She believes that each person, in a sense, creates their own God in their life experience, but always one who is present with them, loves them and helps them help themselves through life's trials. She is sure that is repeated consistently, and for doubting scientific minds like hers, that is proof enough that GOD is.

Those who are atheist, might experience a *divine presence,* if they were open to it. It is more difficult to understand how the material aspects of the cosmos can be related to the God that people talk about or the Son of God they are urged to believe can be in their lives.

Mary Bird Young's life was punctuated early by world events and she was, even as a child, aware of them. She grew up during World War II in a US Naval ship-yard town. Adults wanted to hide the reality of world events from their children. There was no way they could in a major ship-yard town. Bombed ships limped home to the dry docks to be repaired by fathers and mothers. And new aircraft carriers and destroyers were built there by them. Newspapers, magazines and the radio did not hide the destruction, that older siblings and other relatives were killed in battle, that any day or night their town might be bombed. Adults were not sure of the outcome of this war in the Pacific until its horrible ending with the use of the atom bomb on Japan seventy years ago. Only then was the war anxiety for adults and children lifted

That brought in another era, the cold war and hostile international relationships. Proliferation of the possession of atomic and nuclear weapons was and is still worrisome. But it has had a positive outcome. World fear of the use of such weapons and their terribly destructive forces has been a deterrent to its use. It has not prevented a series of smaller but serious and bloody conflicts with no winners, however. But most of the world's people have lived these seventy years in compromised peace in a conflicted world.

It seems to Mary Young that despite many being oppressed by despotic governments, there has been progress in many countries to be benevolent as members of a world society. There is more care from every country to those places in need, differences are more respected than in a century. Distribution advances, and charities have abounded. There is hope for a happier, healthier world.

During her childhood members of her family were deep into Christian Science by Mary Baker Eddy and she was steeped in that belief. She learned to think of the attributes of God and of Jesus as a teacher. She early rejected this faith for its denial of sickness and refusal to use the science of medicine to aid in healing. She saw believers suffer, when relief was available. But her belief in a benevolent deity continued, though shaken again and again.

Loving science, Mary, in an amateur way has a background in it. She has a Bachelor's Degree in Science and has acquired knowledge through her interest in physics and cosmology. The physics professor in college was a Methodist and reconciled faith in God with natural laws. He was a mentor to her and other young students. His name was Dr. Anton Postl, and he has made a significant impact on her life. She also earned two Master's Degrees, one in teaching learners who need special assistance in acquiring basic skills. She taught visually impaired children. Being a speech and language specialist, she also taught children with hearing losses. Her other Master's degree in counseling enabled her to counsel adults and children facing emotional issues and learning difficulties.

"Led into a teaching career by working at an elementary school as a librarian and secretary when I was a senior in high school, I was able to get a scholarship to a teacher's college and was teaching thirty one third graders when I was still twenty in 1954. I did not retire until 1987. By then I had a BS, a master's degree in education and one in counseling. After retiring from teaching I volunteered for ten years as a small group leader of personal growth. I was a counselor in the Steven Minister program at church and a peer counselor with Senior and Disability Services in Marion and Polk County in Oregon. People have been my life. I raised two children and have five adult grandchildren and two great grandchildren.

"My goal as the writer of <u>ALL</u> is not to tell, but to lead the reader into deep contemplation of extreme opposites as a means to understand the nature of problems and the ways to solve them. It asks the reader to question as a means to find solutions to problems."

*"**ALL** has been a process. It started with no plan in site by me, but to write the experiences that led me to believe in the ever-presence of GOD. When I began to see that my writing was becoming more than just journaling, and that I might even self-publish and distribute it, I asked for Divine guidance I believe some of the writing of **ALL** came through me from a higher intellect than mine because I was open for that guidance. But I soon realized that sometimes when HeShe was guiding, I was choosing not to listen. Then I, like a reluctant kid, would find something fun to do and avoid the work. But there was a persistence to it and parts have been written and deleted over and over, as I was on a contemplative journey of my own. It sometimes wrote itself. Hopefully that was when I was paying attention."*

"This book is as significant and as unique as I am. I know that never was there someone quite like me. Nor will there ever be someone like me again. What I have experienced equals a quantity and quality of learning that cannot be duplicated. The awesome fact is. That is true of every human being and every single form of life! **Seeing life from a unique point of view, each has something to offer that no other has! I offer this writing**.

"It takes much from many to give everyone a chance to use the creation that is themselves. I have been given a chance from parents, my grandmother, teachers, my marriage, my health and energy, my country, so I can use the skills and knowledge I have to write this.

"Although I am realistic about what I propose for the Earth, it probably rings too utopian for a place where there is persistence of sins of commission and omission and goals of "ALL for ME and MINE." Is it laced with fear to think of change? What will we give up to act on the "all for all" sentiment?"

Observing the challenges people are currently facing the author fears the acceleration of disrespect, antipathy and selfishness seen in ordinary society. However, the abhorrence felt about the extremely cruel behavior becoming common place now, motivates everyone else to want to do something about it. The question to be answered is: What?

ALL is meant as mental preparation for the human tasks ahead to preserve the wonderful life that exists on Earth. New ways to accomplish that are being pushed into everyone's awareness now. It will require all peoples to change from acquiring and wasting to saving and sharing.

"The good news about reaching that ideal is that, if mankind does not destroy himself and Earth first, there are up to five billion years to reach that epitome before the Sun devours itself and becomes a gulping Black Hole." Let's hurry? Yes! People do devour resources and many people have perished into a black hole, a grave, already.

*"The hope in __ALL__ echoes the song, **Imagine** by John Lennon from the sixties. (To review the words search for it online.) How many years and bad events ago? I've seen in my life-time from 1933 – 2016, however, a rapid change in Mankind's attitude toward a world society with common values. Strangely I have also witnessed the extreme opposite. In the middle of the two extremes there must be a united choice that could change from mass extinguishing of life to the advancement of life. To me that requires the good-will and respect of individuals toward all other people.*

We of the Earth

We of the Earth, who own it by birth,
have a choice now to make for everyone's sake.

Do we want only greed and strife to succeed?
or to share in our life and care about need?

The choice is right now, if time will allow,
to think it all through and change what we do.

By Mary Bird Young

HOW *ALL* CAME TO BE
By Mary Bird Young

There was a spirituality class for women at the Episcopal Church. Richard Rohr's book Falling Upward is the text used for this study. The discussion around it inspired me at the age of eighty-two to do some heavy thinking about where I am in the aging process. I also started writing some of my thoughts down to clarify what I was thinking. I have always liked to write, have not published anything, but began to think I would be serious about writing and maybe it would lead to a published book. I began to write notes toward that goal.

I had long been struck by the awesomeness of extreme opposites like:

Peace>>War

Significant details come to mind when I contemplated the continuum between those extremes. My thoughts began from the most restful and joyful peace with its soul- searching appreciation of others and went from there to the discourse, disagreement and rankling that begins a division. Then gradually it accelerates to out and out war with suffering and death of people drawn into horror and hell. From there with tremendous sacrifice "peace" begins again.

I started writing about extreme opposites in an attempt to understand them. It puzzles me. In between them everything comes to mind, as one becomes the other in an essential, sometimes cyclical way. They are a source of analytical mind activity.

That led me to think and journal about my faith and non-faith in God. So I was propelled through the war years to my "get and do" stages into now a spiritual one with belief in God as a Devine *Presence.*

I read my journaling and thought that what I wrote might lend helpful insight to others who question, because I have been in life a long time now and have had time to learn and think things through. People have been my life. The good and bad nature of intelligent people - old, young, rich, poor, despicable, wonderful, nice and naughty - has taught me. I learned from mistakes I made and experiences I had and books I read. I want to communicate what I have gleaned.

Old people are filled to the brim with wisdom and know how. They are a valuable resource that is often discounted by younger, busier people. Society needs their input. Like the Deity, they need only to be asked.

Many have to accept living without their life partners and not being included or consulted in the whirl of society. Their lives become purposeless and lonely. They wait to die. That is when a prayer like, "Help me help myself, God?" brings inspiration with creativity and satisfying results.

I was plagued with having an ever-increasing problem with remembering names, where I had put things, and what day it was. My attention span was short and wandering, retrieving the right word was difficult, time management and organization skills were nil. I felt irritated and often lacked patience. Driving in traffic and driving at night was a nightmare. For safety I gave up driving except for day time and I avoided driving in town except on familiar routes out of the traffic. My husband is losing his vision to age-related macular degeneration. We walk often and hire a driver when we go to a city. We want to stay in our home and hire other help, if and when we have to.

It was time to check out my memory loss with a neurologist. My mother had suffered from short-term memory loss. My brother has had severe dementia for five years, and noticeable problems for a few years before that. I thought my family and my brother's family could profit by knowing, if possible, if Ted and I might be carrying a gene that could affect later generations. With the leap in knowledge perhaps there could be help for those who might carry that gene.

I went to a neurologist in early October, 2015, who said my problem was mild cognitive impairment. He could not definitely diagnose Alzheimer disease, but he recommended we move into a residential home so we wouldn't have to drive and I wouldn't forget food on the burner.

When asked, Bill told him I usually do. True, but I also have burned food since I was twenty years old. When I said that I had trouble finding his office and didn't have much directional sense, he recommended that neither of us should drive. He prescribed a 28 day trial of Aricept. I could renew the prescription once and he wanted to see me in two months. Aricept is a medicine that increases brain function for Alzheimer patients.

It increased mine to the extreme immediately! I liked it! I became attentive, and organized which I had never been in my entire life. Grandiose ideas sparked in my mind, I became compulsive about writing and wrote two "best sellers" in shorthand. They have both been rewritten on the computer and not under the influence of a drug.

One of the books is _ALL_. The other is **Power Steps to Language**. It is a manual about how to engage with a child as he or she goes through the stages of learning language from new born to an independent learner with good speaking, writing and reading skills. It is soon to be self-published. If the reader wants to know more about my tripping out on Aricept, that episode is continued under the section **Back from the Edge.**

I went to a second Doctor about my memory problems who said that I was quite normal and did not have Alzheimer or Louie Body dementia, although I have age-related short memory loss for an unknown reason. Good enough for me, so do many of my older friends. It is a nuisance and embarrassing, but I can live with it.

And then it happened that pains I attributed to angina sent me in an ambulance to the hospital. They did a CAT scan. It showed no heart-related problem, but did show a shadow on the pancreas and a need for an MRI. The MRI showed a pancreatic tumor. A new era of life began with the threat of what that might mean. It could either be benign or NOT!

I told a friend at the church about this news. My friend asked if I wanted to be on the prayer list. That was a few days before Christmas.

I thought and said, "Well it either IS or it ISN'T. In my experience God does not stop cancer." I did not want to waste any life I had left being fearful, so I asked for prayers that I would be calm and accepting as I waited to know results of an exam of the pancreas.

An appointment was for January 27, 2016 for An Upper EUS (endoscopic ultrasound) at Oregon Health and Science University at the Digestive Health Center in Portland, Oregon. I did not receive the conclusive results of the biopsy until February 7, 2016.

With prayers and support from friends I did stay calm and I was busy rewriting this book. That was a five-month wait to see if I am mentally and physically healthy. The happy result. **I am!**

At eighty-two I have a new perspective of what life should be. If I am not too busy now just joyously living, I plan to self-publish at least three more books. I have in mind a book full of short stories for one. **Power Steps _to Language_** is already written. The other is a mystery - even to me, as I have not yet thought of it.

How to Read <u>ALL</u>

<u>ALL</u> is written differently in several ways. Two or three words will be typed together as one. They combine two conditions or attributes into one. Two of them are Earth*life, and* manwoman*kind.* Most important of all are the italicized words because they describe the qualities of divinity like: *life, love, spirit, soul, mind, intelligence and truth.*

This is a book demanding contemplation. It is a book of questions not answers, intended to be motivation to thought, change and action. It is best read with a pen to write in margins or in a notebook. It can be a record of your thoughts. Use a thesaurus to find your favorite extreme opposites.

The author knows it suggests ideal outcomes, but to her they are reachable ones. They are not outcomes reached magically, quickly or simply, but with united choice, sacrifice, extreme effort, motivation by necessity and desire for survival! GF means go think it through. Many sentences end in question marks. She knows they are distractive. Let them distract long enough for some heavy thinking.

Acronyms appear in the text when the writer wants to participate in how the reader is responding. An example is: LOL! Which means laugh out loud because the text is sarcastic, just teasing, or maybe funny? Or it could mean "WAKE UP!"

Then there are the <<<<<<<<<◇>>>>>>>>>> which usually mean "Think of everything you can between one extreme to the other, stop at the diamond to see what is right in the middle. That seems to be where the choice is. Each arrow is a signal to do some thinking. Studying extreme opposites is a major part of **<u>ALL</u>**. Sometimes they are abbreviated: Here><there. Arrows can go either way depending on one's thought process. It's a different experience to think back the other way than how you just did.

Here is an example: Nothing>>>>>>>>◇>>>>>>>>>ALL

Think about the creation of the universe on this one. Think from its beginning to today. What goes through your mind? Write it down. It might take the rest of your life. LOL

Or think of having nothing to having everything you want: Then reverse to having nothing again. ALL>>>>>>>>>>>>>>>>>>>><<<<<<<<<<<<<<<<<<<<Nothing.

Some would go through a mental trauma of losing things as they think at each arrow of losing something. Where the arrows meet in the middle one's thinking makes a change. Then things come back. When in going from left to right do you feel you have lost too much? There are many ways to contemplate the change from one to the other. Look at each thought as you do this. It can be profound!

Another fascination in this book is creating a kind of chant, prayer or mental meditation. Below is an example for prolonging the singing and breath sounds like: s's, r's, l's v's, f's, h's, m's, n's, r's, and z's to form a word. The following orthography is the sentence "Laugh out loud."   LaaaafffffffffahhhhhhhhOOOTLLLLLLoooooUUUUD.

The only way this orthography can mean anything is to concentrate on the sound and meaning of each prolonged word. The purpose is to slow down a reader's mind to think deeply about the meaning of each word. Saying them out loud is fun, too, but most people will think you are crazy unless they join in. LOL!

The writer cannot think of God as a he, she, or a person, but as a power with many attributes she uses HeShe as a proper noun and HisHer as possessives. Some powerful attributes she identifies are: *life, live, intelligence, sprit, soul, mind, energy, nature.* She uses the word "HERE" to describe the *Devine Presence.*

Now March 16 2016, as I do the last editing, I wish I had changed the orthography of He to HSH to represent the masculine and the feminine qualities of God, and I wish Him and His were written as Here for his and her. It is too late to change them now as the manuscript is being sent to Amazon for self-publishing this afternoon.

He=HeShe=HSH= "HUSH."   HimHER and HisHER= "HERE."

"HUSH! Listen and know that I AM and I AM HERE."

Other symbols in the book are:!, 2, 3, 4, 5, 6, 7, 8, 9, 0, [,], \, ;, ', ,, ., /, 1, 2, 3, 4, 5, 6, 7, 8, 9, 0, -, =, [,], \, ;, ', ,, ., /, They look familiar because they are on any key board and mean what they usually mean. Good luck! LOL!

Then there are the >>>>>>>>>>>>> <>>>>>>>>>>>>> which can be used on a Bell curve which is the distribution of a condition on a certain population of people, or situations. It shows what percentage of the group possess a certain characteristic (from extremely few that do to extremely few who don't). It is a way of thinking from one extreme to the other, and is statistical. Google, Bell Curve for information about % of population without adequate housing.

Home>>>>>>>No Home

Mary Bird Young pledges proceeds from **ALL** after expenses will be given to Habitat for Humanity and to research and treatment of dementia.

ALL
By Mary Birdie Young

These are the first paragraphs of this book and also the last. They hold the **goal of** *ALL*.

Factions of religion, politics, and governments cause strife among Earth's people and divide humanity into **We/They,** *and the Earth into* **Ours/Theirs.** *Are they barriers made by the God of ALL, The One God by any other name, Your God – The God of me, mine, of us, of them, of Earth – of Life?*

From space Mankind sees a gorgeous blue, green and white Earth. It is their **Earth***home looking healthy to sustain Life. The planet has only natural geographic divisions. Can humanity change the unseen human chasms that threaten to rip and destroy?*

Religious, political and educational leaders of the world must come together and agree on the natural human values that **Unite.** *Preach them, teach them by any medium that sends God's message.*

People are weary of conflict and seek the Truth. They will recognize and hold it. They can put aside dividing differences, and respect cultural and religious ones that reveal the paths taken by a people.

With the guidance and sustaining Power of the **One***God of everyone humanity can let go of resentments and be one* **Human***kind in all the Creation.* **Each***one* **can work with** *purpose for their welfare and the welfare of others and enjoy the bounty of Earth.*

Then people can let go of resentments. With the guidance and sustaining Power of the **One***God of everyone.* **Each***one* **can choose** *to work with purpose for their welfare and the welfare of ALL on their* **Earth***home.*

Inspiration

Why do I persist in writing this book? It is with God's direction and guidance, I think. I am compelled because HeShe has been a *presence* in my life always. In fact I willingly give my Creator my life as he gave me life.

But lately my faith is tested again by the hurtfulness done in the world, the natural disasters, and the terrible diseases. It is personalized for me as I watch the unrelieved suffering experienced for years by my brother and others who have dementia. They are people who in no way deserve to be punished. It leaves me asking the same question many must ask. Why doesn't God, the Power in the universe, stop these terrible situations?

So this writing has been a process that has been propelling me to find answers. I have found some that reinforce my relationship to a *personal deity.* There are other questions and answers for each one of us to find. Maybe ALL is a start for that.

It takes much from many to give someone a chance to use the creation that is themselves. Given a chance from parents, teachers, my marriage, my health and energy, I can use the skills and knowledge I have to write this. So I have to write this!

When working at an elementary school as a librarian and secretary as a senior in high school 1951, I became inspired to be a teacher. It was like a calling. I wholeheartedly wanted to do it. I was able to get a scholarship to Oregon College of Education and was teaching third grade when I was barely twenty-one in 1954. By then I had a BS. Later I earned two master's degrees in education and counseling.

I was having some health problems in 1987, when I was fifty-four years old, and so I retired after 33 years of teaching. In retirement I was a small group leader at church and in a personal growth program. I also volunteered with Senior Services for ten years as a peer counselor to elderly people. I was beside both of my parents and several others through their deaths. By then I had five grandchildren to keep me busy and happy. People have been my life. I raised two children who are great adults and are now grandparents. I have five outstanding adult grandchildren and two great grandchildren.

Homes
Habitat for Humanity.
*No Home>>>>>>>>>>*People help to build their own home>>>>>>>>>>>>>>>>Home

As you think from No Home to Home perhaps you picture the hovels lived in by victims of wide-spread poverty. They are made of any piece of thing that can be scrapped together. Often large families live there sleeping as they can in rows on the dirt floors. The mothers and children spend most of their day seeking unpotable water from places far away and carry it on their heads back to their home to cook outdoors what meager food they have Their governments care nothing for them and squander their resources to make a few people rich.

What others did you visualize - those four and five thousand square feet homes on the hills of wealthy nations over-looking meagre homes below them? Can't they be a priority for those who work hard to earn them? Without taking away the adequate and fantastically beautiful homes, how can mankind fashion a system where everyone has adequate shelter? What kind of ethics, government, economic system, and educational opportunity best enables everyone to help themselves?

When you bought this book, the writer pledged to give proceeds for research and prevention of dementia and for Habitat for Humanity.

Our Planet Home

So far, through all the giant telescopes placed around the Earth, and even on satellites, no other planet has been observed to have the ideal conditions for Earth*like* life. ***Could Earth be unique for harboring advanced life forms that can acknowledge and communicate with the Creator? Then is Earth*life* not rare, precious and irreplaceable?***

It still is unknown if there is Earth*like* life on any of the countless number of planets and moons that look like they might have that possibility. We know what is here on Earth and it is awesome and needs preservation now. Maybe the Earth is completely unique. We don't know, but to anyone living here it is presently the only home available and the lessons already taught and learned about how to sustain healthy life and living is what must be relied upon.

The Sun and its planets are located in a far edge of the Milky Way Galaxy. The Sun's most well-placed planet is Earth. Probably this region is relatively safe for continued existence. It could mean, since the Earth is perfect for human life, which it is unique among billions and that God's Earth*children* are most precious and treasured by their Creator.

Exploring and learning about all that there is, is an unquenchable human trait and will be done. The outcome will probably be some pioneers going to another planet to live there. What's the hurry for mankind to save itself and the Earth? Anxiety can be put off for several billion years possibly.

Don't jump off the Earth yet! The Sun is not due to burn out for five billion years, which is the final curtain if nature takes its course. But will human-made devastation stop before the sun burns out? Is there still time?

The space program will continue to change human life forever. How many billion frontiers are there out there? But it's a long time coming that Earth*kind* can find another planet compatible to Earth*life*. It must be many decades into the future that migration could take place. Time goes slowly when one travels fast, so will those going get younger? All centenarians will volunteer! Or the other way around. Let's send frozen fertilized human eggs. Most Earth*lings* are probably willing to take a chance to stay here hoping for "heaven on Earth". It seems best to take care of the Earth*home* they already own.

Extreme Opposites

Micro>>>>>>>>>>>>>>>>>>>>>>>>>>>>>>>>>the most enormous

None>>>>>>>>>>>>>>>>>>>>>>>>>>>>>>>>>>>>>>>the most

If you are thinking about these extreme opposites, you will be experiencing some deep insights. Between extreme opposites is found all situations, conditions, emotions, directions, shapes and sizes, materials, esthetics, dynamics, scientific truths, speeds, lights, waves, tastes and colors – everything one can possibly know or feel.

There becomes an awareness that two extremes are inseparable like two sides of a coin and can't be separated because they about one category- like size, shape distance, a quality or location. One would not be recognized or understood, if something was not known about the other. There is a mystery about the relationship of extreme opposites that if understood would perhaps answer questions and lead to solutions in living life fully.

These will be sprinkled throughout the book for you to reflect on them. It is possible to reach some new awareness or even solve some problems doing that. Hard to explain, but I find them rich in meaning with understanding greater than my own. They seem to be cyclical, too and one turns into the other. Between two extremes, an inquiring mind might find profound answers to deep questions. It might even work like a mathematical equation?

God is Here

When people face sudden difficult times they seek help from others, and from a place within themselves or from the *all intelligent Divinity*. Isn't it when we are weak that we find *strength?* In anthropology there is ample evidence that it is part of human nature to seek a *spiritual power* outside themselves. People find over and over that *spirit* answers.

With the willingness to seek the *energy, caring* and *intelligence* of the Creator of ALL as guidance, is there anything that human beings cannot do together to provide for themselves. They have Earth's resources in a sustainable way if they choose to.

To have a healthy, honest population, can others allow millions of people to be locked into poverty seeing no opportunities out of it? Can others help provide opportunities? Everyone must have worth-while purpose in their lives that rewards them. Being a participant in a government that cares about its populace is essential.

It is in the nature of man that they have attributes that they have always recognized in a *higher being*. If they dial in, they can know how the *divine attributes* are theirs. They can access their own strength, creativeness and incentive. Do economies, even governments change when people do not have to suffer and when everyone helps themselves and others? Isn't it good economy, when everyone is productively helping others and themselves?

I AM. >>>>>>>>>>>>>>>>>>>>>>>>>>>>WE ARE.

Small>Large=ALL.   Here>There=Where.   Now>Then=When.
I awoke this morning with the above formulas in my thoughts. The concepts they express are unfathomable to me. ALL, everywhere, all of the time. Take time to see what they mean to you - To me they equal the Creator.
Near>>>>>>>>>>>>>>>>>>>>>>>>>>>>>>>>Far
Think, just as an experience, from **close** to **far**. Man's description God is often that he is omnipresent. Slowly contemplate each arrow to gradually push him farther and farther away until **far** - to imagine him far and distant as many people must believe any God to be. Others are unaware and don't conceive of HimHer at all.

4

Now think! God is as far away from your consciousness as he can be. **You have to make choices to acknowledge that he is nearer to you. If God is always present, isn't it only you choosing that allows you to even think that he is far away?** Take each arrow step that brings him nearer - then farther. This is only an exercise in your perception of where you think he is? What keeps HimHer far, near or *Here* where you are?

What God does is to be with persons to comfort them in their isolation, encourage them and lead them to accept what is. When a prayer asks HIS/HER'S *nearness*, isn't it answered? His spirit and energy is strong in helping mankind to help others and to help themselves – even, or especially, unto death and - beyond that?

Knowledge

There are many ways of knowing. Watch a human baby in its first two years. Their absorption of knowledge is phenomenal. How do they do it? They are aware.

Someone comes to mind out of the blue, the phone rings and it is that person calling.

There is a knowledge explosion. Electronic devices make it possible to disseminate accurate documentaries that feature the most knowledgeable people demonstrating and discussing any subject material. The productions are interesting, attractive with pictures and are up-to-date and accurate. Anyone who wants to know about anything can find information on an I Phone that they can carry in their pocket. If children would be diligent and focused enough, from their home they could have the knowledge it once took four years of college to receive. Learning goes on throughout life.

Strength and Courage

Life>>>Death

Both good and bad conditions are inherent in life, and we are not abandoned by the love God has in any circumstances. He is in love with each one and will give strength, courage and empathy to each in good situations or bad ones. There seems especially to be a *spiritual presence* at the moments after someone dies.

Is death a bad circumstance always? Doesn't it give a way out of a bad situation and into something better? Friends and family members cry in despair and grief, when a love one dies of prolonged illness – but besides that it is relief that that dear person no longer is suffering.

Death is the final curtain on Earth. One who knows they soon will die usually find that it is excruciating that they will not experience future time on Earth. People seldom find it an unbearable emotional experience that before they were born there were eons of past time they did not experience?

Isn't it peculiar to be upset not to experience a future that is unknown? The past before we were born was eons of time not experienced. Seldom, if ever, does anyone grieve that they weren't present then. What they grieve is that they will not see the loved ones they know, maybe never again. If they have faith that they will, it is much easier.

What is after our Earth*life* can't really be known. But it is known that when HisHer *presence* is acknowledged, *love i*s there and gets people through unto death and beyond. There seems especially to be a *spiritual presence* of that person after they die.

God gave Man*kind* choice. Is it whatever choices, even one person makes, then that can destroy Earth and its life? If one or two leaders can decide to drop a nuclear weapon, which is perhaps the unhinging of the Earth's path around the sun, then "yes" could be the answer. Can fear of such nuclear devastation continue to be the deterrent, as it has been for seventy years now for any leader using such weapons?

It takes courage for people to live in this world today and to go about their business with strength and knowledge. It is essential for every voter to be well informed about leaders. It takes respect for one's self and for all people in today's world. Highly egotistical leaders are not great leaders. Only concern for one's own welfare is not enough for today. If all would use God's *guidance* it would be security in a dangerous world.

It takes knowledge, courage, and strength for leaders in today's world to make wise decisions. They must have and continually seek knowledge of what situations are out there worldwide. They must have courage to be leaders in these difficult times. They must have strength to resist quick, unintelligent, unilateral decisions. It takes knowledge for an electorate of any country to select leaders.

One evening I stopped to get gas in a town just west of a pass across the Cascade Range of mountains in Oregon. As I sometimes did, I called a friend who lived there. She met me at the station and while we had a bite to eat, the dark sky became darker and the wind picked up and threatened to be a severe vector storm.

My friend insisted that I not risk driving in heavy rain, but that I come and spend the night. She and her husband in their late sixties have lost their home and savings recently through a circumstance not of their own making. They live in a small old mobile home on a farm and struggle to just get by on limited means. They own no home of their own, although they both worked for over thirty years to ensure their security.

Still they are extremely caring and assist everywhere they can in life. That despite their own poor health. They are people of Jewish faith and keep a positive outlook. If any people deserve better than what they have, they do. But hey are grateful for what they do have.

Beside the bed they made for me, I found the poem **When.** It can be found online by searching on Google for the first line, "When things go wrong as they often will." It described courage and expresses well how my friends deal with life problems.

It contains extreme opposites. Also it contains the truth that we have no guarantee that we will not suffer and struggle in life, but when we do we are not left without the resource of our will to help ourselves and an attitude of hope for a change. I think my friends are strong through God's *empathy and presence.* They know how to go from the difficult in life to doing what they can to reach an acceptable place and be grateful there.

The emotion on the left are what people in stressful situations often feel. Through faith and optimism it becomes possible for them to move toward the right to an opposite feeling. Probably acknowledging what they feel and why they feel it is the beginning stage of reaching the opposite emotion or action.

Wrong><Right,
Down ><UP
Low><High,
Sigh><Smile,
Discouraged><Encouraged,
Stop><keep on going,
Doubt><Faith
Strange><Understood,
Don't know><Knows
Failure><Success,
Lost>Won
Slow><Fast,
Inside out><Right side out,
Far>Close
Hard><Easy
Worst><Best

Choice

All lifeforms reflect God in a special way, **for all can move and have their being**. God as the Creator has *freedom, intelligence, power and will, and choice.* In creating humans however, HeShe gave up some choice over them because HeShe gifted them with the ability to choose what they would do. And though God could renege and take it away, God doesn't. The result of that is that he has no control over what men and women do, unless they wish to make contact with HisHer *counsel.* God is *ever-present is here,* so that is always an open possibility for manwoman*kind.*

What to say about the hatefulness that human beings can and do choose? If there was a devil, that would explain evil. But when *Life, Love, Energy, Spirit, Soul, Power, Intelligence, Mind, Space, and Time are ALL in ALL,* is there a place for a devil? Evil comes within the choices manwoman*kind* makes.

In addition to disasters caused by natural laws of motion, magnetism, chemical reaction, it is one's own choices which bring pain, injury and death. Though it is circumstantially difficult, bordering on impossible, each person can absolutely govern what choice they make between options. If help is sought, it's easier.

Today the option each has is fast becoming: choose to sustain life or choose to destroy life. That is because the choices human*kind* make on Earth hold the possibility of the destruction of Earth and Earth*life.* It's bleak, but within reach are solutions.

That each life has the power to choose is a given. God cannot control how they choose, but can influence them and others to make wise choices. Wise choices usually protect their health and lives.

Human seeking is a requirement to have a relationship with God. It is not one-way or enforced. It is choice. A person must open the circuit to complete the connection that is always open by God. HisHer commitment to being present in guidance is always there.

Every person proclaiming faith in God and Christ that I have known, believes God communicates and guides them through prayer. It is an experience that many know is real and steadfastly repeated. The connection with a *Power and Love* greater than mankind's own is proven through experience. However, If God always and forever gives men and women choice, isn't it up to them make the connection. He does not force them.

When men and women choose to open themselves to God's attributes they receive from them. Much then can be accomplished that God wills.

God does not create evil. Human beings do by what they choose for themselves and against others. But doesn't hurting others come from a deep hurt, a wound in the psyche so gaping that one is willing to exercise any amount of retaliation in an attempt to heal it? Isn't it the result of Neglect, victimization, abuse, teasing, bullying, and isolation?

The knowledge and information explosion now means that mankind can solve many problems that once guaranteed their demise. One huge problem remains. That is that mankind is given choice by his creator and often chooses what is not conducive to his own welfare or the welfare of EARTH-LIFE.

Attitude

In a world that wants to help people who are misfortunate, the result of helping can make individuals helpless. Also it's dangerous to do too much for children. The attitude of "I am entitled" gets out of balance with "What can I do for myself and for others?" The attitude of "I deserve" results in someone being very self-centered and having difficulty thinking of others. They are also irate when they don't get what they think they deserve. Then they blame everyone except themselves.

Individuals who are only given to and are expected to give nothing back are not happy. They find it difficult to have confidence and self-worth. They often look for someone to blame for that feeling, too. Then comes bitterness against others for the situation they put themselves into. If they had had to help themselves to get along, they would have.

It is hard for them when they see themselves as the center of everything to recognize that they aren't the center. That others count, too. If they do finally acknowledge that they do contribute to an interpersonal problem, the best words they can say for that are: "Help me, help myself?" (God, the person with the problem and other people can hear that loud and clear. They are ready to help that person help themselves.)

Other renditions of the same petition are: "Help me help them? "Help me help him? "Help me help her?" "Help us help ourselves?" "Help all Earth*people* help themselves?"

Having a positive feeling that everything is really OK seems to promote health and welfare. But does it also prevent people from looking closely at reality? GF! Can one have a positive outlook and get into the action of solving problems?

Do some religious beliefs lull us into a comfortable place? For example the Christian belief that we are saved by faith in Christ? Does it mean, "Just wait for the rapture? Others maybe will suffer and die on a poorly maintained ***Earth***home while we go to heaven." Many question if that fits God's loving nature, and doubt if that is what Christ meant by what he said. Also how many knew years after his death, what he meant?

Pessimism>>>>>>>>>>><>>>>>>>>>>>>>Optimism

Realism>>>>>>>>>>>>><><<<<<<<<<<<<<Denial

Apathy is an inaction somewhere in between

Is it difficult to be an optimist in today's world if reality is acknowledged? It is comfortable to deny or avoid knowing about the negative reality today with all its looming problems? What will motivate action? Is it realism, pessimism, optimism or all three?

Motivation

Sometimes the more there is to do the less motivated people are. Why? Maybe because it is not easy to see that what they could do would make a difference. They are discouraged by the burden of so much to do, they want to give up.

A CreatorGod who created men and women to reflect HisHer *intelligence, energy, spirit, soul, life and love* gives those qualities generously. In prayerful asking and expecting direction there is a renewal of energy and with 24 -7 – 365 days a year each is given there will be will be plenty of time for men and women to get the important things they want to have done accomplished.

Those who accomplish the most are sometimes labeled "genius". They might not really be smarter than many others, but with the same time as anyone else they are motivated to work hard and they know how to make the creative shift to use the *intelligence* they know is there to help them.

Natural Laws at Work

Consistent laws exist in a system of creation>destruction>new creation>life. Falling happens, crashing happens, wind and fire happen, floods happen, heat and cold, wet and dry, expansion and contraction, electrical, atomic, magnetic attraction and repelling. Life experiences the results of them. Why would a loving creator not stop them to prevent injury and death of those he created and loves? These are laws of nature that have to be consistently there for order. Choice as a given seems to be a natural law, but it can lead to either order or disorder and it seems to alter what Creator**God** can what HeShe wills to do. It must be a covenant God made with HisHer Earth*creatures*. Covenants are not broken by God. So God must understand when we must make hard choices.

All Powerful God could change natural laws to save lives in peril, from natural powers but he does not choose that. The laws of physics that direct gravity, chemical reactions, and warm air rising and cold air sinking, water flowing, magnetic pull or momentum would be broken and all would be in peril. God does not cause destruction everywhere to help each person in jeopardy.

What HeShe has done is create life to have built in protection in their bodies and good intelligence to avoid danger. What HeShe does do is help men, women and children help themselves and whenever circumstances in the natural order invade HeShe is there to comfort even through death and beyond

There is *natural order* that comes out of extreme disorder. A relationship is between two opposites. One comes out of the other and sometimes it cyclical in the natural order of things.

This cycle is clearly apparent to anyone who does the dishes or cleans the car or house. LOL

Order>>>Disorder

Disorder>>>>creation>>>>>Order>>>>Disorder>>>>>>Order

In the cosmos when the core of a massive star's fuel is consumed the star expands into a super nova perhaps light years in size. It's intensely brilliant light is seen billions of light years away, the brightest of the bright. In final heaves it furiously explodes, giant fiery streams spread debris, toxic gas, radiation and star stuff in every direction. There-in are the building chemicals that appear in matter and all life. Then it collapses in on itself, capturing even light into its exceedingly black hole. It is the future of our Sun in about five billion years. By then our progeny will occupy in peace billions of planets.

In multitudes of other galaxies massive cosmic entities collide there in destruction. This and other violent activity is among billions of stars and orbiting planets. Masses are attracting other masses while the entirety is spiraling around a gulping black hole. All this we recently have learned, is laced with micro particles or waves of "dark matter" that make up as much as eighty percent of the mass weight in the universe. As yet it is not known exactly what it is only that it is through and throughout the universe.

So where do people experience God's strength? When I think to connect with Him-Her-Here, I feel a quiet, calm d*ivine presence* guiding me, *comforting* me, and *caring*. All of nature and the new knowledge about the universe or universes is thrilling in its violent dynamics, so unlike the God*presence*, I know. So I question sometimes, *gentle* God's place in it and even whether God is a Creation or the *creator*. In some way is *divine power* a catalyst that makes it happen, but is unchanged? How do tiny particles become immense entities of chemical, electrical, atomic, magnetic *power and energy*? How are mortals made to be able to even think about such immensity?

The hymn "How Great Thou Art" expresses well my sentiments here. Find it in the United Methodist Hymnal or the lyrics are on line to be Googled.

See the miracle of creation and wonder at it! It is barely comprehensible and is indescribable in anything but lengthy mathematical formulas. Yet some men and women are understanding and learning to explore the cosmic. *Creator* of Earth, and Life releases the information to those who choose to seek it "Here" through HimHer. If Men and Women can do that, can't they also make this planet beneath their feet livable for eons to come and explore others, too?

There is no guarantee that any other planet will be compatible for all Earth*life*. To continue to live here on EARTH is likely to be mankind's only option. Which demands mankind to continue to promote healthy life here on the planet we all own? How much time do we have to do it? NOW is the only time there is. Right? Yet predictions are that when the Sun burns itself out in five billion years Earth will be devoured. That give us some future.

There are unstoppable Laws of the Creation, and in laws of sustaining Earth and the life forms on it. God's plan is to equip human beings with strength in their bodies to be able to withstand or avoid danger. A person who wants a long, healthy life does not put themselves in the way of destructive forces. There God might not be able to save their mortal life or save them from injury.

Choice is a social law. Society does not work well without it. It is the basis of democracy. A despotic government tries to thwart it, but it can't really be stopped. There are choices available in all situations.

So is choice an unbreakable law like gravity that is always in operation? It is powerful. Individuals, groups of people or entire governments and Manwoman*kind* collectively can and do choose cruel outcomes for themselves and others. The Creator would never allow his creation such sorrow, if HeShe could stop it.

By giving life choice, the Creator has limited Hisher choice to have the lives HeShe has created do and be only what HeShe chooses. Freedom even unto human beings destroying life is a given. But the wonder of choice for men, women and God is that human beings are given the freedom to decide as individuals or collectively to ask the help of a loving God to assist them in promoting the welfare of others. He leads them in the way to do it. It results in the creative inventiveness of Manwomen*kind*.

Education and Knowhow

From here on in this book I, Mary Bird Young, will state my thoughts without asking many questions. Whether the reader agrees or not is their choice, of course. In dialog I would ask their opinion. Writing this book has been a long process of questioning and serious thinking. I do not have answers, but I share my firm beliefs and ideas and hope that you share yours with others for I believe out of dialogue there are often solutions.

Human beings have the capability, energy and the power to know how to solve most problems. **There is a continuing information explosion. Whatever is knowable can be known. Opening the conduit through which information flows from the *great communicator*, God of All, enables inquiring people to partake of** *knowledge.*

The Bible especially in the Western world is the source of much inspiration and comfort. The content of it stretches over thousands of years of human life. It cannot be discounted for its history of human endeavor and the covenant that was made between ManWomen*kind* and *God* through the ages. Though this author has not read them, other books that form the basis of religious belief must be this same inspiration for much of the Earth's population. Within them in places are found the same basic *ethics* – for there exists common *divine ethics* that when followed build good societies. God is described as loving.

Also within the Bible, and in other books from the past are incredibly cruel and destructive directions thought to be given by God. Carried out they were and are cruel and unacceptable in any society today. Such acts are a recipe for resentment to continue through a long history. They do not represent any description of what God or man is. They might come out of deranged minds of someone from that set of history, mores and circumstances.

We are helped by God to defeat disease, but microbes are life and life was given choice to be and do what it does. So sometimes life is out of control. However, in the scheme of life is protection. It comes to play every moment in the way life is created for illness to be defeated. *Creator*God made our bodies to heal themselves. He leads us to make choices to have good health. He guides doctors and scientists to learn how to use medicines and procedures so our bodies can heal. There are miracles of healing. The medical profession has learned how to aid the body systems to perform them. It is through God's *knowledge* that it is possible. When it is not possible God *is present in his capacity to lend compassion and support.*

God's power can only be available when a man or a woman chooses to open their connection to their Creator. Each person has control of that through choice and covenant. It seems that God's will for human*kind* comes with their choosing. A covenant is a promise made and kept by two. A covenant made with God propels one through hard times to do his will. The Creator's will is powerful and benevolent to men and women. Every covenant made between God and a man or woman helps God help human*life.* Covenants are not to be made in vain. All promises are work to keep!

To believe everything in the Bible literally is lacking in proven knowledge. To home or church school modern-day children that everything in the Bible is true is, in this writer's opinion, neglect of their education and is delaying it. To believe as an adult that the Bible is accurate is ignorant. It also is insuring that faith in God will be compromised by disappointment.

But to teach the historical stories from about how people in the past lived and believed is helpful today in understanding human behavior because humanity hasn't changed much since then. It actually is comparatively recent time since the advent of human beings.

If the Ten Commandments were followed today, it would be a kinder world. It is tragic that ethics and ways to treat others is for many children not taught well in all media and all places today. It's quite simple "do not do anything that hurts someone else, including other animals." It is taught and learned in nursery school – then often forgotten.

Don't hurt others>>>Hurt others

Help others in life. >>Don't help others.

Cosmology

It is a surprise to our cosmologists that billions and billions of enormous stars, galaxies, suns and planets plus everything else are speeding faster and faster in all directions. With all they know of forces, that was not predicted! So why? They do not know!

More than eighty-five percent of the universal weight and mass is made up of Dark Matter. They call it "dark matter" because it cannot be seen. It's God's big dark secret and mystery. Some imagine it might even be HimHer and it is called the "God particle" by some.

Astounding as this sounds, some scientist are seeing that the equations that describe processes would indicate that everything comes from nothing. It is appearing that the whole material universe was in a ball no bigger than a grapefruit before it was so compacted, hot and active inside that it exploded and presto in 13.7 billion years it is the whole universe speeding ever faster in all directions. How is that possible unless matter is made of mostly nothing? Good each galaxy and its members kind of hang in together!

Most of the human body is "Dark Matter". It is in and around us and everywhere. The most informed cosmologists on Earth do not know what it is! Doesn't it need a more exotic name? How about *"essence." Da*rk energy could be "push." Then there is no confusion. So much dark and black is confusing.

They do know Dark Matter is there, weighty, in abundance, throughout everything. The biggest machine ever built, the Hadron Collider, has been accelerating protons toward each other while pictures are taken every second to determine what particles appear when they collide. Great efforts are being made to find out what they are. Some headway has been made because they have seen particles from collision and recognize one they have not seen before.

But what does it mean? Something very profound formed seconds after the Big Bang. That explosion from extreme compaction of matter resulted in the release of all matter in the universe. Learning what Dark Matter is receives the ultimate in inquiry and there will soon be a break-through promising to be revolutionary. Then like learning anything else, there will be more to learn.

The energy and inflation of this universe is immense. It is violent to the extreme! It is creation in the extreme! We have little trouble thinking of God as *life.* Stars a million times larger than our sun exploding, and gulping black holes sucking up everything near, including galaxies stretches the imagination. Our galaxy, the Milky Way, has a huge black hole propelling everything into a spiral. But how and what is God in all of this?

There are 100,000,000,000+ stars and they have planets, too. In the Milky Way alone and there are billions of other galaxies. Light waves going 186,000 miles a second travel through space and time for light years and appear in our large telescopes from a time 13.6 billion years ago. Collisions through attraction of one mass to another occur regularly. But still perhaps the Earth is unique as every person on Earth is unique.

Science books cannot be written fast enough to give current information on discoveries. The laws of nature are continuous and constant, but some about micro particles are baffling and inconsistent with what's known of larger entities. What is known about God is through connection made with HimHer *presence.* What we know about God out there in the dynamic universal chaos and order is mystery and miracle.

Change

Collectively it's Mankind's choice that can bring peace and care for the Earth and each other. Not easy considering the base nature of Mankind. Is it possible to correct what it is that doesn't allow humans to live harmoniously with each other? Is it hopeless?

Among a large population on an "isolated" planet this old woman says to everyone "Go figure it out!" Then come together with ideas and means for **change.**

It requires a pervasive shift in thinking and values. Change requires sacrifice of what has been tenaciously held as all important. People resist it. It starts with choice. With the power and love of God, is it possible?

It seems there is evidence that through the Creator's use of natural selection and mutation people are becoming more benevolent and more intelligent. If so Earth has a chance to heal from mankind's abuse. There is a paradigm shift in collective attitude, too. More people rich and poor are benevolently dedicating their resources to promoting a better life for others and often with their seeing of God's *guidance and support.*

Homosapiens appeared on Earth some two hundred fifty thousand years ago. Cumulative learning has brought them to today. But for thousands of years they were able to do what most people couldn't do today – that is live completely off nature; finding and fashioning from basic natural materials everything they needed for survival! They were not unintelligent.

Maybe people today are more like those early people than they are like the people of the more near future who might be much more able to accomplish peace on Earth than human beings have ever been.

To make this all work well for Earth the human population cannot grow beyond the Earth's capability to produce for it. With the present birth control methods it is possible to reduce population slowly. It really won't reach that unsustainable place if conservation and care of the EARTH continues. A maintainable number of people will prevent poverty and it would reduce the number of deaths of the young and allow people to live longer.

Some changes on Earth and for People come quickly. Sometimes in evolution it is the result of a sudden beneficial mutation. Having observed groups of children over a sixty-five year period, the increased incidence of autism is astounding and maybe alarming. Socially they have a difficult time, but I have noticed some of these children can learn some things very specifically and show talent in their pursuits. For learning information these are positive characteristics.

Some of the most intellectually inventive people who've contributed greatly to the arts and sciences have shown some of the same characteristics. People do seem to be becoming smarter. The knowledge and inventiveness of Manwomankind has become explosive.

This writer wonders if autism started as a mutation. Could the increase in numbers of autistic individuals point now to an ever- increasing occurrence of a gene influencing higher and more attentive intelligence? I am not a geneticist. But no other answer has become apparent and the incidence has increased dramatically. It seems that many are offspring of very intelligent parents. More research is necessary. It's probably more than one condition not all children labeled "autistic" have the same characteristics.

Didn't many of the highly-contributing inventors, musicians, architects, scientist, doctors, artists, philosophers, and writers in human history have some characteristics that enabled them to shut out distractions and go into deep concentration? Those who have contributed much for the benefit of others are often called saints or geniuses. They knew how to connect to the *intelligence* of their *Creator*, didn't they?

In my brief eighty-two years I see a change in the very nature of people. Perhaps is a genetic one that enables them to more easily choose to be kind and caring and to want to cooperate to sustain a good life for people on Earth. Compared to the eons of time since homosapeins appeared on Earth, the time since Christ has been very brief. He influenced a huge change. But also it is quite possible that more change will be initiated by God. HeShe creates in rapid ways as well as gradual and natural ways.

Even though there are terribly hurtful choices being made and we hear about them continually on media that emphasizes that kind of reporting. They still are by far the exception. Most people are kind and caring and want what is best not only for themselves but desperately for others, too.

People are not happy without freedom and purpose. People build no confidence in themselves or pride of accomplishment if they get everything they want without making an effort.

Out of choice comes **change**. Solving a problem first requires wanting to solve it. The same old behaviors and habits seem to work well enough that to change them brings fear of the unknown and resistence to change. The first resolution comes with the acknowledgement of the problem. Then when people engage God's *help*, HeShe gives it. There must be the acceptance of the help, which is not magic or miracle, but through dedicated hard work sacrifice and time.

Solve the problem. >>>>>>>>>>><>>>>>>>>>>>Don't solve the problem.

Between the above two extreme opposites are: over population, no understanding between factions, resentment that carries revenge, helplessness, inadequate governments, despotism, monarchy and greed. Are these solvable by human beings with the skills and technology of today and HisHer's help – "Here's help".

16

On Earth all fellow human beings can reflect the *love of God* and all his other attributes: *energy, spirit, soul, intelligence*, and so much more. Then will needs of anyone be unmet? How does manwoman **change** their nature so that they can do that for others? They need the will to do it. No one is helpless in it. It can be a united effort for the world's billions. For the preservation of Earth and Life on Earth, doesn't that **change** have to happen?

Information

Christ was the example of a man who could love others irreversibly. Can God change all people to be Christ*like*, through their choosing? Manwoman*kind* is competent to make life on Earth peaceful and good by acknowledging God and letting HisHer wisdom influence them to change. If people can do that, they will be worthwhile and worthy to go out into the cosmos and populate other worlds with their *care*. Perhaps already God has created a home for them out there somewhere.

To accept what God does and what he doesn't is essential in having strong faith. All children, and all are the children of the Creator, need to realize what God does and what he doesn't. HeShe doesn't do what human beings can do for themselves. He doesn't change natural laws and do extemporaneous miracles.

He does give *love, courage, support and direction* as humans decide what to do and how to do it. Today with new information about the immensity of the creation in both the micro and macro realms, some people are not secure in their beliefs. Information is overwhelming and the security of believing what they were taught is gone. Those who found security in believing the Bible literally, now can't and their faith in God wavers. The wavering leaves many unable to seek help from a *higher being* for they wonder if one exists. For others the awesomeness of what they are learning reinforces their faith.

Different religions of the World reflect distinctive expressions of culture set in time. Values learned at one time in history are carried through from generation to generation. Stories of faith that rewarded integrity have especially been told and retold to help men, women and children of each generation work for sustenance. But changes have taken place more rapidly in societies in this century's more recent decades. The old stories do not seem relevant to present day young. Many do not attend churches to hear how seeking a *higher power* can help them. Their parents don't either or make worship a part of family life.

The world has so drastically changed that although the stories have value historically, they do not attract the interest of most of today's people. Immersed in the troubles of modern life, they are needing relief and understanding for how to conduct themselves in these challenges. If they ever go to church they might not receive that from the pulpit if what they hear is how someone centuries ago dealt with their lives.

On page 29 are listed ways that religions can and do assist with helping people find ways to work together for world peace. They are still the source of providing education and ways to change human behavior toward harmony.

Human beings have the capability, energy and many have the educational opportunity to develop the knowhow to solve most problems. There continues to be an information explosion. If whatever is out there is knowable, people can choose through their will and effort to know it. First they must choose to open the conduit through which information flows from the *great communicator*, God of All. With HisHer will, it will be done on Earth.

Convincing the world's people to be a United World People solving world problems together requires dissemination of information, leadership, and change in thinking, mores, ethics, traditions, practices, and preferences – a paradigm shift. Such a shift requires GOD's *will* and the will of his creation, men and women. It is advocated and being done today. Those who give themselves to unselfish goals find it fulfilling and will do it again and again. However the choices of some people committed to selfish goals sabotage the work of others..

Unselfishness is there to learn, unless a person continually chooses to think that they are the only important person and everything should revolve around them. Many despotic world leaders have thought exactly that and some have killed millions trying to prove it.

Because we are made to look at life from our point of view, we all tend to put us and ours first. God can change that, if a person chooses it in *covenant* with him. However self-respect and love for self are important in order to love others and respect them. It has to be balanced to get along with others. If one does not acknowledge undo self-centeredness as a problem and seek God's wisdom to mend it, they cannot participate in the satisfaction of sharing required in a peaceful world.

Many of the extremely competent and extremely wealthy individuals on Earth are sharing themselves, their knowledge and wealth to assist others. To name a few, Jimmy Carter, Bill Gates, Opra Winfrey, George Clooney, Warren Buffet, everyone who ever gives to a charity - there are many, and it does not make them poor in any way – it enhances them.

Those who work in social fields like medicine, nursing, education, psychology, psychiatry, teaching, are intensely sharing their love with others. But so is anyone doing service for others. Older retired people are volunteering in communities by the millions not even asking for pay. It's happening now with our Creator's guidance. If everyone took better care of themselves by stopping the bad health habits and disrespectful behavior many public dollars would be saved for advancement of human*kind.*

18

Everyone needs a hand up from others sometimes. All need to ask themselves what they can do for others. Then everyone fortunate and unfortunate would have what they need. Each can ask someone and their God to help them help themselves and following the guidance of God each person would be a bonus for world welfare.

Teach>>>>>>>>>◇>>>>>>>>>Learn>>>>>>>>>>>>>>>>Do>>>

Young parents are overly taxed by the demands of earning a living, acquiring a home, education, employment, raising a family. It takes the employment of both mothers and fathers to earn enough to maintain their homes. Children often do not get the guidance they need to become good citizens in a crowded world. Dialog urging compassionate behavior is lacking.

The past is important to know. It prevents the repeating of practices that do not work for the population's health. Dogged adherence to mores that resulted in suffering must be acknowledge and stopped on a global scale. It can be done through education and consent to change.

Unheard of truths are emerging from a huge information explosion in all areas of science. The education of our children must keep abreast of it all. Knowledge is necessary for them to do the thinking that will allow them to add their creativity to the best to that body of knowledge and make progress in keeping a good life on Earth for everyone.

Sexual mores and practices has led to overpopulation which results in failure to thrive for masses. Over population means that the collective needs of people are beyond the resources of the land, production and distribution. It results in sickness, suffering and death especially of children, while their mothers watch in the greatest agony on Earth.

Education of both females and males to change sexual mores and prevent conception is essential. Adequate birth control methods can be available now for all people on Earth. It means making it a world-agreed-to commitment to provide them and the education in their use. Both men and women must choose with understanding to use them over watching their children suffer and die. Consensual change of sexual mores will result in reduction of birth and make it possible for a healthy sustainable population on Earth.

Both men and women must take responsibility and have only the children that can be adequately cared for. Until a child is wanted and can be provided with a unified family, the place to control population growth is to prevent conception. It is entirely possible in today's world.

It is the sperm and the egg that results in conception? For many males the sex drive is totally free to function whenever and wherever to the exploitation of women and suffering for them and their children. That has to be addressed everywhere on Earth with establishment of agreed-to consensual ethics. It requires the knowledge and cooperation and strict ethics of both males and females. With that sex is to be enjoyed. Without it is a bane to women.

Should any child who is not wanted or cannot be adequately cared for, be conceived to suffer through life? Today people do have a choice of whether to conceive children or not. Few, if any women will chose to conceive a child they cannot or do not want to take care of. Men, too, do not want children to suffer, but it is a challenge to consider that over the natural sex drive. To have a healthy society responsibility in reproduction is essential, so overpopulation where people have education and resources to prevent conception. In a modern world those resources should be **freely** available. Why aren't they? GF It is not a cost issue. An unwanted child is ultimately a huge cost in every way much more expensive than birth control training and items. It has to be a priority for every religion, government and adult.

Most people are appalled by abortion. If "Right to choice" clinics excluded abortion and were called "Right to Prevent Conception" clinics, would solve the abortion objection and greatly improve the advocacy for preventing unwanted conception.

There needs to be clinics for men and women to learn and be provided with free birth-control items that prevent conception. Both sexes need attitude adjustment and education about how to be healthy, sexually-active people with respect for each other.

Abortion is a separate issue. It would be rarely needed without unwanted conception. There is no reason for unwanted conception where control of that is readily and freely available. It should be the primary government give away. It is totally practical for maintaining healthy populations. Every lifeform on earth reproduces in vast numbers and results in over production of the species if not controlled, as in the case of humans it is controlled by massive deaths. Do human beings want that for their species? Enough children will always be born to maintain populations because it is natural to want children. Those who do not, should not have them.

When abortion is the most positive solution and sometimes it is, it cannot be tied to "Right to Prevent Conception" clinics. It requires screening and matching of perspective adoptive parents with a baby's biological background. Counseling for healing of abuse, genetics and grief are important. Hospital stays might be necessary in some incidences.

If it is a religious issue, the minister or priest could be available also. The woman carrying the child along with a caring father make the ultimate choice. If those two disagree, it is a woman's choice. It is not the choice of a religion, or the government. Even God cannot or will not make that choice.

Natural Disasters

Coastal lands are increasingly being flooded and ravaged by storms, earth quakes and tsunamis. In the future they might not be the place for dense population. With continued global warming, large exodus of people to inner continent locations might be necessary. Would such a change be possible with man-womankind's concerted effort starting now and continuing if necessary. It would perhaps be more desirable than to continually repair infrastructure and buildings in large coastal cities.

Isn't the Earth large enough for all life to live in harmony and abundance? Especially if we continue to have only the number of children that can be given a safe life and good education.

Every continent has land in its interior that is under-used but has fresh air. Which is not even a resource present on most planets of our sun or of other stars millions of miles away. Solving a water problem and building closed-system green houses and making underground homes with sun light and cooled air could open many hot areas to livable ones.

Why dream of other places when we are here on the unique planet with resources perfect for Earth? The world's people can develop the technology with ingenuity following the guidance of a *loving GOD's infinite intelligence.* Use of solar energy, innovation for air conditioning, desalination and purification of water, greenhouses, underground dwellings, and industries unique in all the Universe is on Earth for sustenance of harmonious human life? Every lifeform born on Earth has co-occupation rights on it and responsibility toward it.

Now climate change is real and so is drought in many areas. It's a huge problem but is within capability to solve it with ingenuity and united effort. There is plenty of water on Earth. Isn't it possible to convert H2O into water? LOL!

To spread water over vast acres of land takes more water than is now available. New ways of conserving water can be found. There could be a huge improvement in the life of millions of people. Children could reach their true potential. Everyone could pursue happiness!

The industries of all countries can be environmentally friendly. Methods for disposal and recycling is possible for waste and sewage now. The renewal of infrastructure is essential and new methods are more practical than the old. There would be no unemployment or lack of purpose in anyone's life. Everyone's' efforts would be needed. Without expensive defense systems being necessary every country would have financial resources to do what is needed.

The elderly and sick can choose no prolonged suffering when their bodies no longer sustain them. God provides in death a benevolent escape from suffering and a path to a better life. **Life** can provide loving comfort and care through that process.

21

Basic Ethics

The people of the world can insist on a revision of the United Nations that would not allow one nation to ultimately veto what is agreed upon. The UN has agreed on Human Rights. The world's people as a whole have not, therefore crime, and fraud abound. The following procedure could help emphasize anew a world commitment to a simple rule for conduct.

The majority of Earth's people probably agree on what ethics and behavior works well for the welfare of everyone. However as a way to emphasize that and do away with trivialities, particularly on which the religions of the world differ, a process of getting consensus and commitment on what ethics are most important from the World's people could be devised.

Here is an example of a process:

1. Ask for God's help in organizing a strong United Nations as a world advice court forcing governments to uphold a process to determine a basic ethic on which all people agree. Set aside by the United Nations an "Earth*people's Week*"

2. Each adult in each community would meet together sometime in that week in groups of about thirteen to agree on a basic ethic that, if everyone complied, would bring no harm to them from other people. Selected by consensus it would be expressed in as few words as possible.

3. A responsible scribe would send or take it into a larger community center.

4. All the selections would be perused and ones that were alike or similar categorized together under as few words as possible. A group of thirteen would by consensus select only two to send to a larger center.

5. This process would be continued up through cities, provinces, states, countries. Until each country sent in a compilation to a representative group. This group would be no more than one hundred people representing the major religions, an outstanding educator from each level, a representative from the field of psychology, political science, the medical field etc. They would select one brief description ethics on which they could reach a consensus. It would ensure that people are not hurt by other people. That one to be put forth as something all people could commit themselves to follow. Ultimately a United Nations would agree to enforce that ethic in every country with united agreed-upon consequences.

Utopian? Impossible? Yes, but possible! What would unite people to get along as a world*people* without hurtful conflict? Maybe belief in a benevolent God who assists people to do HERE's will when they "want to want to" and ask *I am HERE* for help.

22

Most people, when they seriously think about it, already know what social behavior works. Religions particularly agree, though they let themselves differ on minor issues and instead of working together work against each other in competition on issues of past dogma that have little to do with GOD's truth.

Leaders of the world's people would select in consensus the ethic selected by the world's communities. In all no more than one hundred top people. Their assignment would be to find the essential ethical law that they ALL agree upon (in consensus). One that they each can make a public commitment to uphold as a **world order**. Then the people can agree to live in peace. The simpler and the most *inclusive* ethics possible could be agreed to. Like "Do no harm to Earth or Earth*life*."

Then all would agree to have an organization of United Earth's People with representative from all nations to uphold that concept, and be an active advice government in assisting all people to have resources and education to care for themselves on a local level.

God's Nature and Cosmos

Here is a subject of complete mystery. People often think of "God" as synonymous with *life. If God is life and God creates life is God the creation and the Creator of life?* Everything is not known yet, but most of life on Earth experiences the *divine nature* of God. Maybe tiny microbes don't?

How l*ife* came to be is a mystery, an unusual miracle that maybe can be revealed by inquiry and examination as science is now attempting by looking at the complex protein molecules in life. As the most complex intelligent lifeform, mankind seeks answers and invents solutions. AS men and women question there is a connection made with what is knowable. And that knowledge is available through d*ivine Intelligence.*

So far there is not proof that advanced intelligent life exists in the universe anywhere but on Earth. However the pure chance that it does is great since there are billions and billions of stars that have planets orbiting them. Perhaps, though, Earth and human beings are totally unique. Uniqueness is not rare. LOL Life is so diversified. No two human beings have ever been exactly alike. If so we are supremely precious!

We must preserve ourselves and Earth until at least billions of years from now when our sun is no more. By then perhaps manwomen*kind* will proliferate throughout the Universe and beyond. If so, they will take their *divine natures* with them so peace will prevail everywhere.

CreatorGod is a mystery because the creation is so vast, complex and dynamic for our limited knowing to fathom. But *loving*God is as familiar as ourselves, if our mortal self is put aside and that *presence* is acknowledged. "Hush and know that I am God."

What and where is God? People repeatedly experience that God is in love with Life. HeShe cares about life, is for life - the Creator of Life. The characterization of God's nature relating directly to man is often described in the following words: *"Life, and Love."*

Other descriptions of God's nature as it relates to Earth*life* are *Life, Love, Caregiver, Counselor, Teacher, Psychologist, Intelligence, Energy, Nature, Provider, Guide, Soul and Spirit*. God works on Earth with manwoman*kind* and animal*kind*, too. Earth is God's and manwoman*kind*'s laboratory where the *teacher* is imparting knowledge to the pupils.

As to what man's *personal* God's relationship is to the extraterrestrial vastness it's hard for human mind to conceive. I am awestruck when I look up on a clear dark night and I just wonder at it all - cosmic streaming, twinkling, shining, warping, speeding, spinning, spiraling, exploding, fiery, colliding, expanding, contracting, racing masses. I don't have a clue. Except that it is from whence we came. Every particle that is us is star stuff. God has to be *energy, power, light and waves, and space time*, and "Essence" That is what I want to call dark matter. God in the Universe or Universes is harder to conceive of than when he is with us here on Earth, with attributes we find in philosophers, teachers, artists, musicians and counselors – wise, *full of soul and caring.*

Isn't it good that there is that Mystery at a time of finding out so much information and answers? To not know everything keeps humanity humble and close to God, who does know. But the personal characteristics we reflect like *Life, Love, Soul and Spirit* are not unfamiliar and mysterious. HisHer caring *presence is close, here and knowable.*

From whence did God come? What came first all the mass in the multiple universes or the HeShe we know HERE at home on Earth? What came first? God*creator* or the materials to shape the creation? It's heard that some scientist states that everything can be made of nothing. There is tremendous comparative space between electrons and protons in every atom. So if protons and electrons are *energy,* then what matter is there? Did Einstein ask the same question? E=MC squared?

The humongous mass, one universe was contracted into a small, seething ball until it had to release its tremendous energy. It was a violent, instantaneous inflation that for 13.7 billion years is continuing faster and faster. From that comes the building particles to make all that is? Or is there another source for the *unseen* but very *present*? For example did *caring* pour forth from the Big Bang. How will what or why ever be known?

Little ball>>Big Bang>>Creation>>Inflation>>>Increasing speed>>?

Black holes attract and absorb even light and increase in size so that galaxies with billions of enormous suns and their planet families whiz toward the abyss and whirl into it to be sucked into where? Probably that will be the demise of everything in the Milky Way also, sometime in the next billion or two or three years. Better than Disney World! Go think about that, or if it is closer to your heart, think about and solve what is wrong with life on earth and fix it.

So I have personal experience in the God-Me relationship. What is hard to fathom is God in the expanse amidst all the explosive forces that destroy and build. Is he a part of the creative forces or created by them? If he is the Creator, how did he come to be?

24

Isn't it like we've heard? Now is the only time there is. The past is a fleeting memory and the future is a dream. No! Time is relative and changes with speed. It's yet to be discovered what life is out there billions of light years away. Human beings do not have to go there to learn about it. Satellite probes are sending back amazing information all of the time even from beyond the solar system. However, if an Earth*like* home is found within reach, human beings will be compelled to go there. It is in their nature to move out and explore. Perhaps even to settle there while the Earth is a maintained home for many.

This book <u>ALL</u> is urging that scientist continue to advance toward sustaining a livable Earth even though they inquire to know everything in space. A good start has been made with a binding world economy, a United Nations and other organizations of people working together. There are dedicated people everywhere who assist others toward their independence. Doctors donate their skills to heal the afflicted and weak and enable them to help themselves. The persons who have been fortunate enough to have fortunes are donating their money, time and talent to the less fortunate. When people are free of want, they can learn and reach their potential for a fulfilled life and join the forces to make Earth the best home it can be for ALL.

Then everyone would be busy and productive. An economic system would be established. No one would be unemployed. Monetary resources could augment from what doesn't need to be done any more - like wage war and compete unnecessarily with other nations The Earth is a closed system. It still has the same resources it ever had although transformed. What is needed for Earth *life* is on Earth.

Cascadia Fault Disaster

It appears there will be increased disasters. Most will be along coast lines where storms are prevalent and there are rising sea levels and where Earth plates push one under another.

By history and observations scientists are predicting a devastating earthquake when pressure from subduction under the continent breaks loose along the British Columbia, Washington, Oregon and California Coasts. It is an eminent threat. When it occurs it will leave thousands of people effected. When exactly will it be? No one can be sure and warnings will be brief. Therefore people need to be prepared. Evacuation and escape from the areas is the only hope to avoid danger.

Government other agencies and churches are now preparing plans for disaster relief in a subduction zone in coastal areas of Western Oregon, Washington, California and British Columbia. There will be earth quakes, tsunamis and floods by the subduction under the continental coast.

If you live near a tsunami prone area, or if you visit there:

    1. Always have in your car vacuum-packed quantities of dried survival food, clothing, sleeping bags, and pup tents. Make them permanently a priority for space.

2. Everyone in your party will have a cell phone and know the whereabouts of the car in which they will leave the area.

3. Keep the car in good repair and always filled with gas.

4. If there are warning sirens, get to the car immediately. Be sure those who will evacuate with you know the procedure to meet you quickly at the car. Urge guests to be prepared in the same way you are. Having enough cars is crucial in a sudden emergency. At the coast it might require a long trip to avoid the disaster.

5. If pets are not with you and it would take precious time to get to them. Be broken hearted, but leave them. Do not sacrifice people for animals or things.

6. Know evacuation routes around bridges and water ways. Go immediately to higher areas. If possible get up to the coast range. Your goal is to get over the Cascades into Central Oregon and then Eastern Oregon because Central Oregon will soon be crowded with many refugees. Even Salem and Portland could become an Earth quake disaster area or be crowded with refugees.

What to pack in your car:
Conserve space by vacuum-packing clothing and sleeping bags.
1. dried meat. 2. Varieties of dried fruit. 3. Nuts and seeds. 4. two gallons of fresh water. 5. Tablets to purify water 6. Sewing kit 7. Flashlights. 8. Soap 9. Paper products (toilet paper, paper towel, wet wipes) 10. Variety of plastic bags. 11. Credit cards, licenses, cash, passports. 11. Nylon back packs and nylon clothing bag for each person 11. Two sets of underwear for each person 12. Spring-fall set of clothing one size too large for each person 13. Winter set of clothing for each person one size too large. 14. Sleeping bag for each person.

Human-made Devastations

The Earth is in peril of some leader somewhere making a decision to use nuclear bombs and weapons already in their arsenals. With probable retaliation, that would be rapid widespread devastation. The destructive acts of two countries can affect the welfare of all countries can't it?

But mankind has been choosing life on Earth which can guarantee that Earth can flourish without a slow continuous route to its destruction.

Now is the time to begin in earnest a plan involving the effort of everyone to do as much as they can to maintain their home, Earth, for lasting livability? Becoming a united people in this effort is the only guarantee. Isn't it? There are only two options. Which will it be?

Never have so many cared so much and devoted their lives so vigorously toward the welfare of others. Today huge amounts of effort, resources and money goes into research to make life better and to insure that the Earth can sustain. There are constant pleas to everyone to give to charities, and many grasp the opportunity.

There has been tremendous strides through science that give us a promise that life can be safe and happy for everyone. Men and women choosing the *creator's guidance*, can accomplish that goal, when it never was in sight before.

Is it unrealistic idealism to imagine a world where everyone works toward taking care of themselves and are dedicated to maintaining a healthy environment for everyone on Earth? Doesn't every person and life form have the same birthright as a partner-owner of the Earth?

Are a small percentage of people entitled to frivolous surpluses and wasting while the majority cannot live adequate, healthy lives? Facts of the matter point to an Earth that cannot continue to sustain any life, if serious problem-solving is not done by everyone.

Mutual disrespect is ever more obvious in today's human society. No need to site all the incidences on Earth that daily remind us of that and gives us profound grief.

"January 1, 2016, in a New Year's address Kim Jong UN the leader of North Korean, reminded the world that he is ready for war!" That's headlines for Earthpeople. "Happy New Year, Earth!"

He is twenty seven years old on January 6, 2016. How did he intend to celebrate his birthday? He exploded a nuclear bomb buried in the Earth! "Happy birthday young man!" May you grow wise and benevolent with age! Today March 4, 2016 He announced he now has a long range missile that can carry a nuclear missile at any time. "Why not become like the Christ who, I once heard, was predicted to appear as the second coming in Korea?"

I stated that question into the air and prayed for this young man. But today February 7, 2016, he sent a far reaching missile into the air and the world watched the people of his country celebrate.

The general world-wide question is: "What is his plan really? Is it like he says just for peaceful purposes? Sanctions are placed against him which he is resistant to address. What is his plan? He says to protect his country from aggression?

Fear of the use of more and more destructive weapons has brought no quick resolution to conflicts. All leaders who reason know that to accelerate l use of weapons to the nuclear, would be self-destructive. Instantly they would get the same back.

The hawk cry of some leaders to use the weapons they have and win their goal could ignite the use of Atomic weapons and permanently alter the livability of the Earth-home of all Earthlife. How can mankind change that? The horror and threat itself has bought seventy years without a world war. But it is a precarious peace with no promise being continuous forever. Is it just based on flawed human*kind*'s **choices**?

Still there has begun a global paradigm shift with a chance for each Earth*person* to make a commitment and a covenant with God. Will people who have the most materially will have the hardest time getting "through the eye of the needle?" It appears not. Some of the riches people on Earth contribute great sums to charity and even go to needy populations and work with the people there to improve lies. They have the financial means to help with the process and especially today demonstrate their willingness to do that.

Hatred and destruction >>>>>>>>>>Care and renewal.

Broken Laws

There are Laws of Creation that in a vast system called the universe, cannot be changed. There are also ethical laws for human conduct that are simple and if followed bring harmony between persons and caring for all Earth and Earth*life*.

Isn't it the villages' responsibility to recognize if someone is likely to be harmful to others and to insure that there are funds available to provide mental health help for them and their families? Shouldn't every child be raised by a community that gently and consistently demands they follow the Earth's basic ethical law? Society can curb the sale of games, media or materials that promote hurting or killing others.

When a vast majority of people are practicing kindness and everyone sees that it is what works best, the profoundly obstinate and wayward, hurtful people will become fewer and fewer. Most of Manwoman*kind* would choose care and renewal!

Still the horrible choices a few make are so devastating. Will everyone ever be whole and kind and live to respect and love others? This is the biggest problem to solve for all people to be safe from a few.

On the current news the parents of the children killed by a mentally ill youth at Sandy Hook are suing the manufacturer for making an assault weapon that had no purpose but killing. It was advertised and sold to appeal to just such a deranged young man. My opinion of this lawsuit! Good! What is yours?

With universal agreement some simple ethics and simple consequences of breaking them could be drawn up by lawyers from various countries meeting together. These laws would guarantee immediate loss of freedom for those who serially or mass kill others. If there is no doubt by witness or definite proven evidence of guilt, there is no need for trial.

Quick dispatch to a facility that provides as privileges: basic shelter, clothing, nutritious food, cleanliness, respect, safety, exercise and labor responsibilities which would give some purpose in being. There should be assurance that person will never again repeat the crime by never giving early release.

The purposes of immediate incarceration and no trial are first to eliminate the media attention sometimes given for years to the perpetrator. This makes the atrocity attractive to others of the same mind-set who would copy for the glory of spectacle. This happens in disturbed minds. These long court cases when guilt is obvious are an unnecessary expense and floods the courts unnecessarily.

This writer believes justice can seldom be done. If someone is hurt by another, hurting them in return cannot erase that hurt. It expresses anger for what was done, but the healing of the injury is only eased through the regret the perpetrator might have for what they did and the sincere expression of that to whom they injured. But society needs to be protected from those who commit crime. Incarceration does that.

The threat of incarceration is a deterrent for people who might take advantage of someone, were it not for them wanting to avoid a record or some time in jail. But a person who is angry and confused enough to want to cause difficulty or pain for others is not deterred by that threat. Punishment and long sentences probably exacerbate a desire to retaliate and repeat hurtful behavior.

There are probably good programs for rehabilitation, or change in a person's feelings of wanting to hurt others. They seem to be missing in most prisons. Regret within the conscience of a person is punishment that leads to healing. Prisons can be denial of any special accommodation. They are a humane warehouse for people who are a threat to other people. An expedient and temporary denial of a privilege for an infringement of the basic ethnic rule agreed to by World committee could be a consistent consequence without being torturous.

It could be a facility that demands respect of one for the other and the upholding of Earth's basic ethics such as "Thou shalt not hurt or kill." If that person breaks the tenants of such a law it is enforced by them temporarily losing a privilege.

In my mind, while watching the manmade trashing of our only home, the injury to and killing of life; if Manwoman*kind* is to survive there has to be unified effort. The Earth will continue to exist under its increasing burden, but will life continue to be compromised with more and more misery. Why would anyone choose that?

All people must aspire from inquiry>thought>paradigm shift>benevolent action. Surely *The* Creative *Power* that brought human*kind* to existence is on their side to guide them and promote life, not destroy it. It seems that resources of *Life, Love, Light, Intelligence, Spirit, Soul, Mind, Energy, Nature, are* available *when* manwoman*kind* **chooses** *to open their connection to their* Creator. *Yes, but all do not yet choose. All we can do is pray to God to help us, help others help themselves.*

Help us, Oh God, whose love we reflect,
to help those who must first ask,
"Help us to help ourselves
for we do such harm the way we are!"
Help us give to them what they need,
to do what they are meant to do.

29

The pressure is on for humankind to collectively find ways to promote Peace on Earth, so war has no greedy purpose. People know that the nature of war has changed. There are no winners. Doesn't agreement to sustain life or to destroy Earth and Earth*life* rationally point to the clear positive option – to sustain Earth and Earth*life?* How can everyone agree to add their effort to a united effort to do that?

There has to be a universal code of ethics shared by all human beings that is very simple and basic. Ask the people. They know. In social relationships that are harmonious a basic ethic operates. If it were universally upheld, like a part of human nature, it would eliminate suffering that comes from choices that human beings make.

Church Role in Public Education

If human beings in successful societies already use common ethics, and all religions already teach them? What are they in fifteen words or less? If we can describe them in simple words for all men and women, our differences become the same for basic conduct.

Every neighborhood has church buildings that are unused much of the time. Couldn't religion's resources, which were established in the first place for the guiding of people to life-improving ethics be used five days a week to educate our children? Wouldn't our children's chances for learning morals and ethics be better taught there than in a crowded public school. All kinds of other skills could be enhanced in small groups within a church?

What about churches? Is there good reason why church buildings cannot be the seat of alternative education in neighborhoods? GF Here stand thousands of little-used buildings. On Sabbath days the rooms are used. Twenty-four six they are not. Property of all kinds is owned by the large churches everywhere. What about our educational system, overtaxed by expense, complicated curriculum, excessive testing and paper work and laws that prevent moral education?

It seems that churches could use their resources for public education. Religions could forego their specific beliefs and teach a basic agreed-upon ethic and curriculum that does not interfere with separation of church and state. In fact if that ethic were basic in the society, financial support would even be possible through public funds.

Churches are wealthy in buildings and human resources. They can be instrumental in providing good education that includes ethical values for children within their neighborhoods. It is often done now for preschool and kindergarten. The best curriculum possible to lead children to the best resources for learning could be available today through a partnership with them and the public educational system.

Ethics and morals can be taught in churches and the presence of God through choice, but not well in public schools that demand separation of religion and state. What a good use for the loving spirit of many retired teachers and others. What a good use for under-used buildings. What a good way for helping parents to be better parents, too. It would grow fading congregations, by attracting families.

With the use of the computer and excellent media, education far exceeds use of textbooks, and long hours sitting in classroom listening to inferior (by comparison to excellent programing) instructional lectures. Excellent teachers must be present to augment these with personal interaction and follow-up discussions and activities.

Starting with a pledge from each student that they agree to uphold a basic but broad ethical law such as "Cause no hurt or harm to anyone. Respect yourself and everyone else." This with a simple brief consequence when it is broken would usually limit the repeating of the infraction.

1. Teach basic skills to help them to be self-learners.
2. Teach library use and library skills as well as research computer skills.
3. Give assignments and the freedom to use all that is in a community to complete them, assist them where needed.
4. Have small groups made up of three-year and four-year spans in individual ages. The older ones assist the younger.
5. Use retired people as volunteer workers for all positions and hire other competent people to lead them.
6. Everyone, including children can participate in the maintenance and upkeep of buildings as part of the curriculum.

There are Laws of Creation that in a vast system called the universe, cannot be changed. There are also ethical laws for human conduct that are simple and if followed bring harmony between persons and caring for all Earth and Earth*life*.

All evidence is pointing now to undisputed global warning, partly or totally caused by the lifestyles of human beings. The areas of the Earth most effected are where the populations exist along coastal area.

Human beings must think of options from now on to save the Earth *home* from being unlivable in the not too distant future. It not then human*kind* loses itself forever. We are worth too much for that to happen. But if my observations are accurate about God having limits in saving us even though he loves us, we have to enlist his help and get busy! Does that entail leaving out some frivolous endeavors? For sure it asks us to use our time, health, and energy in new ways.

Save Our Earth*home*

Save>>Lose

Contemplate this seriously. Save Earth or lose Earth? It is one of the present challenges in the lives of Earth's people from now on because man has done much damage already to the Earth. It can probably recover, but it cannot sustain many years with the present rate of destruction. However, its natural possibility for existence may be billions of years more if that rate is reversed.

31

The Earth cannot be replaced. It likely is unique because of its chemical content, its position in the galaxy, its size and placement in the solar system, its tilt on its axis, its chemical composition, its mass and attraction to other objects, the approach of other objects not on course to collide with it, its nontoxic atmosphere, its oceans, its mild temperatures, its capacity for growing food, its flourishing flora and fauna? Why do we look elsewhere? Isn't cherishing the creation that's here a good idea for most humans? GF!

Earth*Life*>>>>>>>>>>>>>>>>◇>>>>>>>>>>>>No Earth*Life*

Is "in-between" all the things we need to do to save human*kind* from *ex*tinction? What are those things?

Possibly Earth is the only place in the universe with intelligent life. We don't have any proof otherwise. But then if we meet some life kind of like us, maybe we would wish we hadn't! GF I know mankind loves to explore and they will do it. Using unmanned probes without going far seems the best option for now while we fix up the home we have.

Every continent on Earth has an interior with low population and all of the elements that are needed for life, except for easily available water! With today's sense of ecology and industry can a difficult environment on Earth be made into areas of productive living easier than migrating to another planet that probably has more difficult problems to solve to be habitable by Earth*people?*

Coastal areas are already compromised by climate and weather for sustainable living. It is predicted that increases in oceanic volume will continue to submerge coastal areas. Already repair and rebuilding with huge effort and expenditure is necessary over and over as each year the sea level increases as there is ice melt from global warming.

There are other answers. Perhaps it is not too soon to establish some examples of refugee-like communities for evacuation of populations. They could be placed east of the Cascades in Oregon and Washington.

Predictions are consistent with evidence that there could soon be earthquake and tsunami devastation from subduction of a costal shelf under the continental one along the OREGON coast. This would result in mass destruction just west of the coastal range.

Water is the most crucial need for the welfare of all life on Earth. Many otherwise livable areas on EARTH are not livable for the absence of water. Yet our oceans are rising due to climate change. Many coastal areas are under the siege of destructive weather events. Water is everywhere. Making it potable and good for agriculture is the problem. Surely it is possible.

The volcanic Ring of Fire along Pacific coastal areas will be continually besieged by disasters. That is where population has settled and the peoples are threatened the most in those areas because of volcanoes, storms, tsunamis and earthquakes. In time it appears that a resettlement of the masses must be to inland parts of the continents. But the problem of few sources of water there and intense temperatures must be solved by the ingenuity and resourcefulness of mankind.

The following are solutions that came quickly to Mary Bird Young as she contemplated the problems Earth's people will face especially around coastal areas.

Water must first become plentiful. This will require new technology. Isn't it doable in a world where hydrogen and oxygen are two of the most common elements?

Of course, desalination of water is done now. But transporting water distances is a problem, except water does flow downhill! LOL! Diverting rivers would not be an answer for the damage it would do to the environment and economies. This is a good challenge for scientist! Isn't it much easier than traveling light years to a little known planet that isn't prepared for Earth*life? Maybe* in a billion years. Homes can be constructed of insolation material that is easily available (like straw) and can be prefabricated to put together good homes at low cost. In very hot areas they can be constructed underground with good air flow.

1. Air conditioning and light sources. Infrastructure can use wind energy for electricity. Disposal of sewage can be figured out to be simple to do.

2. Each village, town, city can be sustainable with green houses and agricultural practices and seed sources that efficiently grow very good and abundant food.

3. Protein sources are many without depending on meat industry. Cattle can be free to live their lives in ways that do not include their slaughter.
   New carbon free transportation methods can be invented. Every village can have a government that is directed by the people.

4. All of this is economical once there is little need or desire for excesses because everyone can have their needs met in a near-perfect world.
   Absence of huge defense spending would help with expenses. It is likely that repairing roads and infrastructures in coastal cities will not be permanent, as the sea level is apt to keep rising. Evacuation and abandoning vulnerable cities is probably the ultimate answer. Rebuilding with the best technology and materials available homes and industry that meet practical needs with freedom of the populace to grow into their true potential for adequate, fulfilling life.

5. Good birth control would insure that no child would be conceived without insurance that they would be loved and cared for in health and safety.

Why Not? If one person, an old lady with amateur knowledge of science and religion can conceive of these solutions, isn't it possible for highly knowledgeable professionals to come up with workable ideas and procedures for making human life positive for all of the Earth's people? This old lady thinks so with input from the *Intelligence* of the universe. GOD loves his Creation, Men and Women. In connection with them, miracles are made.

33

```
Them>>>>>>>>>>>>>>>>together<<<<<<<<<<<<<<<<<Us
Commonality>>>>>>>>>>>>><<<<<<<<<<<<<<<<<Diversity
Together>>>>>>>>>>>>>>>><<<<<<<<<<<<<<<<<<Apart
```

The following paragraphs are the first and the last paragraphs in <u>ALL</u> because they contain the essence of the book and bear repeating.

Factions of religion, politics, and governments cause strife among Earth's people and divide humanity into We/They, and the Earth into Ours/Theirs. Are they barriers made by the God of ALL, The One God by any other name, Your God – The God of me, mine, of us, of them, of Earth – of Life?

From space Mankind sees a gorgeous blue, green and white Earth. It is their Earthhome looking healthy to sustain Life. The planet has only natural geographic divisions. Can humanity change the unseen human chasms that threaten to rip and destroy?

Religious, political and educational leaders of the world must come together and agree on the natural human values that Unite. Preach them, teach them by any medium that sends God's message.

People are weary of conflict and seek the Truth. They will recognize and hold it. They can put aside dividing differences, and respect cultural and religious ones that reveal the paths taken by a people.

With the guidance and sustaining Power of the OneGod of everyone humanity can let go of resentments and be one Humankind in all the Creation. Eachone can work with purpose for their welfare and the welfare of others and enjoy the bounty of Earth.

Then people can let go of resentments. With the guidance and sustaining Power of the OneGod of everyone Eachone can choose to work with purpose for the welfare of ALL on their Earthhome.

Mary Bird Young

34

Autobiographical Sketches
To Begin It All
By Mary Bird Young

My mother had two sons. She wanted a daughter and named me Mary Joanne Forbes Mingle as soon as she felt me flutter. Now eighty two years later I choose as my "pen name" Mary Bird Young after my mother and grandmother who both showed love to me in abundance and coached me in a religion that I cannot fully believe. But after living eighty two years, I still find it at the heart of what I do believe.

It was an off-season wintery dawning in October in 1933 in the middle of the Great Depression. Hard times did not begin to ease until 1939 and then there was World War II! (I grew up in world historical times of excessive stress.)

It was a time when arctic winds already blew across the vast Flathead Lake in North Western Montana. Another mouth-to feed was not a welcome event for a forty-year-old disabled unemployed World War I veteran. At 6:00 AM in that bone-cold, one-bedroom cabin in Montana my father stoked a wood-cooking stove before frantically leaving to fetch a Doctor. I had put my mother in labor. With no phone, in an icy storm, a car that had to be cranked repeatedly as it bounced, choked and sputtered to a start, this was no easy chore for Dad.

When he came back, he was livid and cursing a doctor who was sitting in a restaurant eating breakfast and said there was no hurry because I was turned the wrong way and labor would be long, but that he would be there soon.

Entering the cabin he heard his wife's periodic groans and cries. He didn't know what to do! He went to the back yard to chop some wood.

At nearly eight AM my tiny Grandma Birdie was overcome with anxiety. She stressed to remember Christian Science truth. I was arriving, but the Doctor was NOT. I am sure her dark eyes shone out of her pale, round face and she wrung her hands that were wrapped in her long flannel nighty.

Suddenly I was free and slid onto the bed, hopefully not all blue and cold. The doctor did come and did what doctors have to do. Though there, I can't exactly remember what. Though I heard that he turned me upside down and spanked me until I took a breath. I later had learning problems and didn't read until I was ten years old. Maybe it was my birth experience and/or the whooping cough that choked me four months later. Whatever, something made for a difficult early schooling.

My mother was overjoyed at Birdie's words "It's a GIRL!" Birdie, as soon as she could, elatedly called out into the yard to my father who was still furiously chopping wood, swearing, not under his breath, at a wayward doctor who'd said he would come soon, but didn't.

"I don't give a dam what it is!" Just so it's here!" He burst out, still angry at the whole dam trouble. He kept swinging the ax.

When he did come stare at the little dark face fringed with black hair he said, "Well, that's a little "papoose." After that, "Papoose," "My Sweet Bunch of Onions" were two of my many names. More were "Babe", "Sis", "Sissy", "Dummy", "Jo", "Joan", "Joanne", "Little Cuss", "Cuz", Kid" and Go Home."

I was born with two people present, Grandma Birdie and Mom, Mary Mingle Forbes. I am as sure now, as they were then, that God with all His attributes was near, too. That is *Divine Truth, Life, Love, Soul, Spirit and Mind*. I heard these words about GOD when I was an infant. I direct my prayers to them now.

I was swaddled and nurtured with the concepts of the divine expounded by Mary Baker Eddy, two aunts, Mom, and Grandma Birdie. From Dad I learned, "take care of yourself!" It is the best advice I've had.

Grandma Birdie's big name was Bertha Hermia Young Mingle. She was all of four feet and ten inches tall. NOT the size of her name. With dark brown eyes, very fair skin and red hair, she fittingly was called "Ma Ma", "Bird", "Grandma" or "Birdie" by her four children, eight grandchildren, and many nieces and nephews. I am the youngest even at eighty-two. My brother, I and one cousin are still living, but likely not long on this Earth.

Birdie was cute. She was widowed at age sixty by my grandpa who died before I was born. Grandpa stood six foot three inches and looked like Abe Lincoln. He was a successful business man and babied her into helplessness. He lost everything they had in the depression left her with no resources. Before welfare or social security she had nothing and lived with her children until she died at age eighty five.

Her religion was her strength and love was her power. When I was a child, I thought she had the fragile velvety soft nature of the fuzzy moths that hung onto the screen at night on summer evenings. I knew I should think of her like the perky, sharp-eyed, birds that hopped around in the trees, but she was peaceful and quiet. I adored her and the moths who had cute little faces.

Christian Science continues today locked in by two books The Science and Heath with Keys to the Scriptures by Mary Baker Eddy and THE HOLY BIBLE. I took serious issue with Christian Science because it denies the undeniable, the reality of matter, sickness and death. The antithesis of the religion is the newspaper The Christian Science monitor that reports world-wide reality in all fields of science arts and news. A high schooler having success in a creative writing class, I aspired to go to Boston and be a reporter for The Christian Science Monitor, but turned to teaching for thirty years. In college I found outlet for my writing zeal as editor of the college newspaper.

My father, an atheist at heart, taught and showed his children, above all things reality. . He told his kids, "Don't believe the "fairy tales" that your Grandmother and aunts believe." We always knew from Dad that there was no Santa.

36

An early scientist in attitude, I needed proof. As a child, I was gathering the eggs on the farm where my Aunt had free-range chickens. Butch, the rooster, named so because he was too valuable to butcher. The rooster, Butch, the usually arrogant aggressor, was wobbling around unable to give any attention to the hens. He looked my way but didn't even run after me to peck, jump up and attempt to pierce my legs with his talons, I knew he was very sick. As hard as he was to love, I wanted desperately for him to be Butch again.

I would defy the disbelief of my father and prove the faith of my Aunt. I fashioned a well-planned religious experiment. If I did, as Jesus and Christian Science taught, I, too could do as Jesus did - heal the sick. I found in the Bible where it said so. I might even grow up to be a CS practitioner like my aunt.

So I held that bony, floppy, feathered-guy close and believed that even chickens were made perfect by God. "There is no reality in sickness and death. Life and love are all in all. There is no room for sickness. This rooster is spiritual not material. Therefore death can be defeated by loving him and acknowledging only life."

But "sick guy", got sicker. He suffered and in a few days in the midst of my diligent prayers, he didn't even flop. He was, no denying it, DEAD!

Faith in the premise of Christian Science was gone. But he was only a chicken. Chickens die by the millions. Dad laughed at my experiment and said since we eat his progeny, he lives on in our tissues. I didn't laugh.

My brother, Ted, and I grew up during the war in Bremerton, Washington. Our older brother, Don was in the US Air Force stationed in Alaska for training to attack Japan if necessary. Our mother who wanted to be a stay-at-home mother with her young children made a sanctuary out of our home. She provided care to infants and preschoolers, neighbor children who had both parents working in the ship yards. Friends of my older brother waiting to join or be drafted into service lived in our basement and called her "Mom."

My brothers were both strong influences for their more wayward friends. Ted's best friend, Rich, was like a brother to both of us. He was a darling, lost boy with an alcoholic mother who abandoned him, his sister and his father. He practically lived at our house during the war years. He and my brother made a pact that they each would marry the sister of the other. I didn't like the idea because I had my eyes on movie actors, like Clark Gable or even Ronald Reagan.

When Rich was sixteen, a popular basketball jock in high school, he decided to play "chicken" on a winding rural road. He drove his car straight toward another car. The first to swerve was the "chicken". Rich swerved in time, but lost control on the curve, went off the road, hit a tree and he and two other boys were killed instantly. I learned about grief and wondered why "all powerful" God does not interfere with choices or crashes, no matter how precious the cargo. I was terribly angry at Rich and God. My faith was shattered. I could not be a Christian or love God ever.

The summer I graduated from high school, a nine-teen year old boy, a friend I adored, who deserved all of everyone's love, died under the weighty bed of a dump truck and I knew for sure, that God cannot stop things from falling, speed and acceleration, bad choices and boys from dying. But I also learned that HE-SHE cared and helped me through horror. I heard Jesus cry with me. I knew then that when the nearness of God is acknowledged, there is comfort and valor. But my religious life was compromised. There was too much written in the Bible and said at church that held little reality for me.

When I attended Oregon College of Education I dated an Oregon State University forestry student and loved him. My senior, he graduated before me. He went to Mt. Lassen forest district in Northern California. Time and distance separated us. When I knew he was a fire fighter, I prayed for his safety. I married but I heard about it when he died in a forest fire. I learned that young men are not protected from fire. "Why, God, why? When I know you to be loving and powerful in my life, can you allow such things?"

I think of Rich, Bob and Ben, grief continues today. I still see their wonderful smiling faces and tear up for what they missed in life and what life missed from them.

I stayed away from churches until my children were born and evangelists were able to convince me that they should be baptized. I didn't want to take any chances for them, just in case my disbelief was wrong about the whole case of heaven or hell! I also took the children to Sunday school a more liberal Methodist church and set the example. They are wonderful generous adults. They only attended church as children never as adults.

I struggled to reconcile my faith and lack of it. As the creator of the universal system, is GOD or isn't GOD omnipotent? It seemed clear he performed no miracles to save a person caught in the way of harm. Unless they occurred in warnings that went unheeded.

Do the laws of nature that have to be consistently there for order alter what the **Creator-*God*** can do? I think that is it! If God changed them to save those in peril, no one could depend on order. Chaos would ensue here and there and everywhere while God helped some. LOL GF. God helps us help ourselves and is there to comfort when circumstances in natural order invade.

As I went through the stages of life of getting and doing, I didn't trust what I had learned religiously as a little child. I discounted the faith of Christian Science, especially when I knew of the death of a child with an untreated wound that became infected. Yet I constantly seek to get back to that pure faith in good by being in a Christian community with those who care about others.

I never could extoll Jesus or accept some of the Bible stories literally as other Christians did. I have felt hypocritical in a Christian setting but I did not feel I belonged anywhere else either. I continued to believe that I could have a direct covenant with a loving, caring entity not at all person-like. I realized I received strength and guidance whenever I opened myself up to Spirit-Energy and Soul-power. In my life when I make contact with *divinity* it is always HERE as in *present*.

Still I cannot believe what I can't believe and I cannot think that there is anything like suffering for an eternity. Was it a way early Christian churches coerced parishioners into supporting the church. Was it even left in the Bible to do that? Some think that is was. How can it be believed that the Bible is the unchanged word of God, when for centuries it has been rewritten by men who can make choices? The Bible has many lyrical, esthetic and touching words of Truth, but it is not a science book or a modern book of knowledge.

Of course, I witness the hell made here on earth by human beings. My mind cannot believe accepting Christ as my savior would save me from eternal damnation while others are abandoned. I do not believe in eternal damnation, but it's anyone's choice.

The rationality is not there for me in many of the Bible stories either. At a time when many questions were unanswered by lack of knowledge, people had comfort and reason from all of those stories, but most do not hold true today and the church loses believers in what does make sense by pushing what does not.

Some of the Old Testament in the Bible is unbelievable accept as history of how people once thought. Human nature remains much the same as it was in the Bible days though and the stories are short and the lessons valid even today.

In my independent, doubting heart I still forget to trust. What a huge amount of anxious energy is expended then! Also what a disappointment if I ever have the expectation that people can fulfill in me what only God can! It's hard on them, too, because I sometimes let them know how they have let me down. LOL!

As a child I thought it was all wrong to call GOD "HE" and to say I was "HIS". It was not true to leave the nature of SHE/HER out of the LOVE that was ever-present guiding and guarding me. Now in my mind I automatically change "he" to HeShe and Him to HimHer. And "here" expresses where we all are. "Here am I, GOD" is one of my favorite hymns.

In the Methodist setting I was and am comfortable being a sinner among sinners trying to make amends and live for others as much as our human natures allowed. There I found my life's friends. Some knew of my inability to believe Jesus was a savior. Those who knew and believed if I didn't accept Him and his virgin birth, I was risking eternal hell, prayed for my soul. I loved and love them and still cannot make my brain believe what it doesn't.

When my children were born in my joy and postpartum blues I knew I had taken part in giving them both life and suffering and death. I took another look at the Christian belief and they were baptized to be sure I was not wrong. It isn't Christ I cannot believe in, it's hell. Though some humans make one on Earth. That hell I see as real.

I struggled to reconcile my faith and lack of it. Is God or isn't God *omnipotent*? As the *creator* of the universal system, it is clear HeShe performs miracles. To save a person or persons caught in the way of natural laws (except in warnings heeded), I see no miracles - only injury and death.

I am a believer in this: There are things God can't or won't do, to protect life no matter how we beg and pray or think we know otherwise. He must be bound by the laws he created. When in life we are sick, we might live>>>or>>> die. Choices made can put us in danger and collisions kill. Fires burn out of control. Things do fall even if a precious life is in the way. So what does God do for us?

I finally know for what it is useful to pray. My rational mind tells me that God is there with compassion no matter what to help mankind help themselves through the tragic times. To ask God to magically save one from the forces of nature while many others perish seems unrealistic and impossible. Those who miss being in a dangerous situation where others are killed, probably were lucky, not selected by God. That is how I believe because I believe each person is treasured by God, and he chooses no one to suffer.

Christians name that *presence* as Jesus. Jesus came as a person living a human life and he understood that challenge and therefore understood ordinary people. I believe he taught mankind to seek a loving God and to respect all people. His presence on Earth advanced the understanding of humanity, so maybe now they can follow his examples and bring world-wide peace.

I do not visualize a human-type relationship in the *divine presence* that I experience. It is *spiritual*. I do not know how to fit Jesus into my life except as someone who taught humankind the best way to live and someone I heard cry with me when I was a young girl. He is called the "The Son of God." I believe he thought of Men and women as the "children of God."

I have attended Christian services throughout my life, without the faith expected. There I learn about God and have had relationships with wonderful, caring people and a relationship with God whenever I seek his presence, which I in the busyness of my younger life did not always remember to do. In this my elderly life I want and do have time for contemplation of my spiritual soul and my relationship to God. I believe I have guidance, when I ask for it.

If we are helped by God to defeat disease, it's because CREATOR-God made our bodies to heal themselves. He leads us to make choices to have good health. He guides doctors and scientists to learn how to use medicines and procedures so our bodies can heal.

There was emphasis on GOD but not so much on Jesus Christ in the Christian Science faith that gave me my nightly prayer " Father, Mother, God loving me, guard me while I sleep. Guide my little feet up to Thee" I much preferred it to the prayer that in the 1940's my sleep-over friends said: "If I should die before I wake, I pray the Lord my soul to take."

I came to see Jesus as a person. A teacher who knew and was *divinity*. He taught people that they reflected *divinity*, too. The examples he gave and the things he did were lessons. The message is that there is one GOD. Jesus taught about him and demonstrated how to be the perfect man, giving hope that each person can be that, too.

As I went through the stages of life of acquiring an education, a profession, a family, and a home I also read many books and thought through my beliefs. I retained much of what I had learned religiously as a little child. I discounted the faith of Christian Science because the practice of avoiding medical help just didn't make sense to me. But being in a Christian religious community with those who cared about others, I constantly sought to get back to that pure faith in good I had had as a child.

I received strength and guidance whenever I opened myself up to Spirit-Energy and Soul-power. Whenever In my life I made contact, I always felt God's presence here and near.

In my independent, doubting heart I sometimes still forget to trust. What a huge amount of anxious energy is expended then! Also what a disappointment if I ever have the expectation that people can fulfill for me what only God can! It's hard on them, too, because I sometimes let them know how they have let me down.

As a child I thought it was all wrong to call GOD "HE" and to say I was "HIS". It was not true to leave the nature of Her out of the *love* that was ever-present guiding and guarding me. Now in my mind I automatically change "he" to HeShe and "him" to HimHer or Here. "Here am I, GOD" is one of my favorite hymns.

In the Methodist setting I was and am comfortable being a sinner among sinners trying to make amends and live for others as much as our natures allowed. There I found my life's friends. Some knew of my inability to believe Jesus was a savior. Those who knew and believed if I didn't accept HIM and his the virgin birth, I was risking eternal hell, prayed for my soul. I loved and love them and still cannot make my brain believe what it doesn't. When my children were infants I tried to and was baptized with them, but it isn't Christ I cannot believe in, but Hell. Though some humans work very hard to make one on Earth.

I am now dedicated to cram the last half of my life into whatever time I have left. I am unique and valuable because I am unique. Everyone and all life forms are like me – they are unique, too!

TED

Primary in my worry-life are deep concerns and grief I have for my brother who has been suffering for years now from the worst kind of dementia. Although I haven't had the care of him, his condition and knowing the struggles his immediate family are having is a heavy emotional burden for me. Ted is two years older than I and we were like twins together. We did our share of fussing at each other as children, but my bond with him is very strong. He is like the other half of me. I have always adored him and still do.

This situation was also impetus for my journaling to help me withstand the pain I felt watching this wonderful person I love deteriorate and suffer for years unable to live or to die. How can I see a reason for it where God is? Who else is for years suffering on the edge of the death of themselves, but these people with dementia? Where is enough funding for this prevalent disease?

When Ted and I were young children we were fast companions. Hand in hand or fist to fist we did everything together. Whatever he did, as the younger sibling, I did. If he came down with whooping cough, chicken pox, measles, mumps, I got it, too. We were like identical twins. LOL?

We went to the same schools to college, and chose the same profession. He was drafted his sophomore year out of college into the army during the Korean conflict. In Colorado he was a leader of cold weather training in preparation for warfare in the mountains of Korea. The conflict ended, however, before he was deployed. But the training was intense, and dangerous, and he has some post traumatic episodes because of it. He has received little assistance as a veteran because he was not in combat.

Together we took care of our elderly parents. Raising our families and pursuing our careers, we were apart quite often. Still he was important in my life. I always have adored him. Cheerful, charming and able to make everyone laugh he was a delightful and kind father of four, a friend and educator to many.

Within the last five years, he has at times been near death and begging for it. I have witnessed life's pain many times, but this is the worst for me. I grieve for my brother continually. I want to help my brother's family, who with love and faithfulness to him suffer, too. I often feel helpless to do anything but cry.

I only know that eventually the brain will be understood enough so something can help others, but for Ted it has truly been hell of no one's making. No bad choice, nothing explains it. It is a shaker of faith, like no other.

An accomplished educator (teacher, principal and superintendent of schools) for nearly forty years, he was gifted in art, home design, construction of buildings and landscaping as well; and was a leader for years in the international Lion's club youth exchange program. After he retired, he was a teacher at Maclaren, an Oregon penal institution for young felons.

This most caring person, he now has bouts of incontrollable behavior. It has at last been diagnosed as Louie Body and other types of dementia resulting in severe impairment of intellectual function. His family finally found it impossible to take care of him in their homes.

He has been shifted from one memory-care facility to another because of aggressive behavior. He was several times been near death and has pleaded to die. But his body is strong and healthy and he recovers to go through it all again. His thinking is very impaired, but at times he comes out with incredible insight and is often like a professional comedian, because somehow his sense of humor is intact. He loves rhythm and dancing. It is when we see him apparently happy that we are glad he is still alive. But he goes through bouts of deep depression, for he is aware of his terrible limitations.

He goes daily from attempting to make other patients comfortable to swearing at everyone and anyone, threatening them and even striking them. He has been to a geriatric center where they kept him several weeks to determine what medications are right for him. Many of them only made him much worse.

Sometimes a care facility has had to call law enforcement officers who handcuff him and take him to a psych ward at a hospital where the doctor does not checked closely what medicines accelerate his behavior and then he is given another to counteract that effect that makes him almost comatose and he is sent back to the care home to wear off the medications which are counterproductive for days.

After years of his and his family's suffering, a psychiatrist discovered that the usual medications given for dementia only resulted in making him physically and mentally worse. She prescribed other medications that resulted in positive behavior and attitude. One is a tincture of marijuana. Laws about that drug still make nursing home administrators reluctant to give even medically-prescribed marijuana because it has not been federally cleared and it can be a legal matter.

Ted's daughter-in-law is a pharmacist and owned a private pharmacy in a small Oregon town. The small community was well served by her. Her husband, Ted's son, delivered to their homes, if they needed that. The people there were glad to have a local pharmacy that cared about them.

Pharmacy laws necessarily are stringent and about six months ago the State board suspended her license and forced closure of the pharmacy. No one, not even she, knows exactly why. There will not be a hearing until August 2016. Charges against her are unsubstantiated and the accusations seem to be wrong and unfair. The source of the complaints about her are unnamed.

Meanwhile she has lost all for which she has dedicated her life. She is working as a waitress. Their bills cannot be paid. They have no heat or lights. Their house is for sale, but until they get money from that, they and a son are literally in poverty. She has had to destroy the pharmacy's inventory of drugs for which she invested thousands. Of course, this causes more worry for the entire family. Ted's prescriptions from his psychiatrist were processed through his daughter-in-law's pharmacy. It seems laws about dispensing marijuana, still federally intact, are the reason for this accusation against her. It is not a legal action it is the pharmacy board denying her practice. No one knows why. There will be a hearing in August, 2016. Many months from the original action against her.

In the care homes in order to handle Ted, care-givers have to be aware of his behavior enough to give him the medication, when he first shows signs of irritation. In memory care units where he has been (Several because they cannot handle him and instruct the family to move him) few care-givers are that observant and the rules of giving medication are to give patients medication only at regular times. So Ted sometimes does not receive the medication before he is out of control and in trouble.

The family has done their best to communicate his needs and are there as much as possible. They are insistent that he gets medication, when he first begins to be agitated and hard to manage, but they usually are ignored and thought to be interfering. It is a nightmare!

Also when he is reluctant to take them, often not much effort is made by employees to make it more palatable or to cajole. Family members visit him most days, but other responsibilities and their own health issues do not make it possible for them to be with him twenty-four-seven.

Because Ted fears most procedures, he refuses showers and clothes changes, and other hygienic care. Employees give up offering him the service because he is belligerent. His family often finds him dirty, ill-kept and with skin infections. They do the hygiene care, change his bed, shower him, change his clothes, and apply medication and moisturizer to his skin. Still it is on their $8,000 a month bill for this care that he doesn't receive. There is little effort in some memory care homes to do anything consistently that is stimulating for most patients. "Memory care" is a misnomer. Most often he and others are just sitting with nothing to do. A TV is on most of the time, though.

So his estate, that is modest, and for which he and his wife worked to accumulate for sixty years is gradually going toward this absence of care. The consequences of this horrible disease for him and his entire family has been dire. It tears me, his sister, apart. I have no recourse to do anything for him, but visit him. We walk and play, silly and giggly like the children we were. I am always glad then that he is alive, but at times when he has been very sill and on hospice and he chooses not to eat and is starving, I hope and pray for his death, but time and time again he has rallied and then I am grateful he is still in my life.

Continued from second page of **How All Came to Be**

Back from the Edge

The reason for my October 6, 2015, visit to a neurologist was that I needed to know the prognosis of some changes I was experiencing in my abilities. That for my own sake, but also because if there is a genetic factor thirty young people and counting in our families could also be affected. Perhaps in the advancing studies in genetics, it behooves us to know about it. My mother showed acute signs of short-term memory loss before she died of cancer at sixty-eight years and my eighty-four year old brother has extreme dementia. I also notice that my smart brain is progressively getting NOT SO SMART.

I know others my age experience that, too. But because of my brother's illness. I was not able to dismiss it. I thought some of the early symptoms Ted has had were creeping up on me. I needed to know rather than to wonder.

The Doctor tested and diagnosed me with mild cognitive impairment. I wasn't surprised. He diagnosed that I do not have symptoms of Luie Body dementia which is what my brother has in addition to other kinds of dementia. His case is complicated and extreme. Because he is very hardy physically nothing takes his life and he continues to live with a terribly debilitating disease.

The Doctor prescribed 28 days of a small dose of Donepezil (Aricept), 5 mg per day. It is used to give Alzheimer patients some temporary extra brightness with what is left of intact brain function. He told me it could be increased after the first prescription and would delay inevitable progression of the disease. He would see me in three months. He recommended that my husband and I get on a waiting list at a resident home where I would not have to cook or drive, and to confer with our adult children about it.

It is a cholinesterase inhibitor. It works by increasing the amount of a certain substance (acetylcholine) in the brain, which may help reduce the symptoms of dementia in patients with Alzheimer disease by stimulating the parts of the brain less already affected. I took the Aricept exactly as directed.

I reacted to it by being exceptionally organized, and focused better than I had ever done in my entire life! I could speed-read and be productive in activity twenty four hours a day. I became quite obsessive-compulsive and reorganized everything in my house in my spare time. I loved how easy everything was and started to write two books. I named one book _**ALL**_ because I was ready to write about **everything!** I wrote it in short hand with many symbols and drawings - some in living color. Within three weeks I was well into writing the two books. I was doing many other things, too. What I was not doing was sleeping!

45

Under the influence of Aricept I continued to write in shorthand the journal I had started. Then I called it ALL because I would write about everything. I came to believe it to be an important contribution to society and worthy of the greatest protections from any destruction. I wrote day and night in the far corner of a bedroom during a windy October 2015. This was the only safe space in our house because the Ponderosa pine across the street swept and bent in the wind toward our house. One in the neighborhood fell on a house, so I wasn't completely irrational. In paranoia I wore a bicycle helmet while I wrote. I built a makeshift safe in the cupboard where I kept my writing and then bought a good fireproof one to keep all of our papers safe.

As a child steeped in Mary Baker Eddy's Christian Science. I was taught that God's attributes are LIFE, LOVE, MIND, SPIRIT, SOUL, INTELLIGENCE Not that I understood them. I still don't quite. I now add **Power, Intelligence, Light, Energy, Mankind, Nature, Space** and **Time.** And what of **Dark Matter and Dark Energy?** I acknowledge the power of each with total wonder. How did it all come to be and have anything to do with me?! Now with this drug I was continually amazed at my own thoughts. But I was not exactly making the connection that it was the drug that was driving me.

In my drugged writer's state I began believing I was only a recorder. The Author, who is the combined powers of the universe, was directing me. _**ALL**_ would be a best seller and translated into many languages. It would be profound enough to change the world!

Feeling insulted that the feminine side of the God of everyone seemed seldom acknowledged. I changed the referents of He and Him. I used the possessive referent Here for HimHer. I used HeShe for the proper nouns. Later I thought it should be HUSH as in "Hush and know that I AM GOD!

I thought of my two dogs as representatives of all animal life and felt extreme reverence toward them referring to them as gods. ("dog" is "God" spelled backwards without the capital.) They received undying attention and I loved them more and more!

I became gregarious when people had always told me I was "too quiet" and thought I was shy. Although inside I was never that, but I always was an observer of people.

I was irritable and critical, when I had been accepting of the roles people put me in before. My friend of sixty four years, fifty-nine years of marital bliss, was becoming more distant. I thought, ready to leave home. I was getting ready to have him do it. 24/7? Too much? = NOT FUNNY!

Day and night I thought about the contents of _**ALL**_. As aide for my concentration I made up the name "Leslie T. Minst" as an acronym with each letter in the name representing an attribute of _Creator_God: _life, love_, _light, energy, identity, eternity,truth, rules, religion,_ _**POWER**_, _mind, mankind, intelligence, nurture, nature, space, time._ I could contemplate silently and slowly each of God's qualities. I made snow trails around my home in nearby woods and in the snow-covered labyrinth at the church. I walked there for hours going nowhere, but far in my mind. I have always been hyperactive and now I was hyper hyperactive! I did everything but sleep for days at a time!

By holding on to each singing symbol in the words I have for GOD there was time to contemplate what each means. It is still a way of worship for me as I walk a snow trail alone. Out loud it might be wonderful, too. *Life, love, light, energy.*

    "LLLLLIIIIIIIF/   LLLLLLuuuuuVVV/   LLLLLIIIIIIIIT/ eeeeNnnnnnnnrrrrrrrrGEEEEEEEE"

I am sure that Aricept for many people suffering with Alzheimer's or other dementias would give much positive help. It would prolong their days or even years of functioning. I do have short memory loss that makes tasks more difficult than they used to be. No one can predict where it goes from here, but I do not need this drug now!

I found the places it took me interesting, but fear going there again. However, it did get me started writing about solving the problems we have on Earth. There was no problem I could think of that I didn't have a ready solution in mind for it! It was awesome to think of so many ways to solve problems, and write it all down. I liked how it felt!

Where ever in the brain such thinking is hidden, this came from there. I heard a psychologist talk about a God center in the brain. I now better know how addiction to drugs is so hard to break. I better understand the psychedelic drug craze of the 60's and 70's, when college professors were saying, "Take it. It makes you smarter."

Though this book was the Creator God's book, I had a myriad of ideas for writing other books. One was a book of short stories. I knew plots for each. One was **Power Steps to Language**. I would home publish it with my computer and printer. It would revolutionize how children are taught to write and read. No child would fail EVER! I already had the beginnings of two novels. I would become a great author!

The outcome was my family became alarmed, when I showed up as the life of the party at my daughter's open house. A forest fire demolished their home in Washington so they had built a new home and had invited all their friends and family to their house warming. Usually in a crowd, I head for a corner and quietly observe everyone's activity. Not this day!

No one could ignore me as I *was* under the influence of Ariccpt, though they wished they could. I was the acentric presence. I never had such a hilarious time, teasing everyone and talking all of the time.

Near the end of the twenty-eight day supply of Aricept what my daughter, who has been a nurse for thirty years, saw me doing and saying was bizarre, and extreme to her. She suspected the medication I was taking.

The book that I was writing looked like scribbles and made absolutely no sense to her. Making my bed on the floor in the corner of the bedroom afraid of a tree falling on the house was alarming. There really is a tree across the street that looks like it could fall on our house. One did snap in the wind and fell on a house near ours. I usually am hyperactive, but I was hyper hyperactive and hardly sleeping at all.

She persuaded me to go with her to my GP. The doctor convinced me I was exhausted from lack of sleep and was close to having a psychotic break on the medication, Ariccpt, which was completely wrong for me. She insisted that I take no more of it.

I recovered completely from the Aricept after a week or two of getting some normal sleep. I looked at the great pile of scribbled notes I had made during my obsessions with being a great writer. I could read my shorthand and it was not so crazy. I began salvaging it and rewriting. I believed it had some merit.

My family and my brother's family wished to have a second opinion about the possibility that Ted and I might be carrying a genetic problem that geneticists of the future could head off. My nephews recommended that I see my brother's psychiatrist who at last has prescribed for him something that helps him. Some of it is a tincture of marijuana

There was a long wait before she could see me. She is a renowned Doctor who ordinarily does not have time to see new patients. However, she agreed to see me because of our family's concerns. I was grateful that she would take her time with me.

My daughter took me to my brother's psychiatrist on November 17, 2015. She is a Doctor, in much demand and especially agreed to see me. Ted, my brother, is an extreme case. She wanted to help me early, if I was developing what he has as he has gone through much suffering and knows medications and what works for patients like him.

She was personable, thorough, intuitive, and astute. She did a complete study of all my medical records. Interviewing me and examining me closely, she found that I performed normally with mild, cause undetermined memory loss. She said I do not have Alzheimer's or Luie Body dementia which is part of what my brother has. She said the Aricept was not for me, I had to sleep and she prescribed something that helped.

So I am the usually hyperactive individual I have always been but having trouble remembering schedules, where I put things and names.

She had some suspicion that I might be bipolar. I don't think so. I have been a patient, peaceful and serene person. I am the usually busy individual I have always been, but within normal limits. I still ride a bicycle, dance or swim daily and have unusual energy for my age. I still notice short memory loss problems, of course, but notice them in my peers also. They are a profound nuisance, perhaps nothing more than that.

It also happened during these months of rewriting **ALL** that pains I attributed to angina sent me to the hospital where they did a CAT scan. It showed no heart-related problem but by chance did show a shadow on the pancreas and a need for an MRI. All this in me, when I felt I was a physically and mentally healthy person. But the MRI showed a pancreatic tumor. It was either benign>**or not!**

Recently one of my dearest friends had died a prolonged death with pancreatic cancer. She fought it with every torturous treatment available for two years or more. Her choice was courageous!

She was in her sixties awaiting the birth of a long-awaited grandchild. She was newly married after the death of her life mate. She had a prestigious place in the community and was dearly loved. She could have had decades to enjoy a good life.

I would probably not do that at my age. I have already been privileged with a long life. I think I would live every moment to its fullest and when I suffered too much to do that, I would choose Doctor assisted help to be released and have my family relieved of a long vicarious torture.

An Upper EUS (endoscopic ultrasound) was done on January 27, 2016 at Oregon Health and Science University at the Digestive Health Center in Portland, Oregon. It was done to determine if I had pancreatic cancer. After another two week wait, I received the wonderful news that I do not have pancreatic cancer! The pancreas is not producing certain endisms for digestion and I take pills before I eat. I am grateful to the pig that produces them. Knowing I do not have cancer has given me new spirit to make the most of every day.

I had waited for this appointment for almost two uncertain months. My church family prayed for my peace of mind during this time and I felt well, usually calm. Rewriting and preparing the manuscript of **ALL** kept me busy. Learning computer skills was frustrating and time consuming. I often mistakenly lost much of what I had painstakingly written. There are still mistakes lurking, overlooked. But I am weary of the process and long to be finished and let it be what it is. Readers beware! LOL!

I came to acceptance of whatever was to be and knew there would be care and comfort for me. After eighty-two yeas of a fulfilling life, each day now is a bright bonus.

Creator God, I thank you for life on Earth and for your presence here. When I consider how great you are, I am amazed that you are attentive to us on this little planet. I want to have faith that this world can be one in dedication to life and the care of our Earthhome. Enable us to be who you created us to be and do. Amen

By April 14, 2016, my writing was ready to send to Amazon and Bowker for self-publishing. It will be on Amazon Create Space and Kindle. I was just finishing my last editing at 4:09 AM. The next day I learned that at almost that exact time my great grandson was born!

The outcome of my experience is the rewritten book, **_ALL_**. I quite sanely believe that when I asked and attended to that guidance, some of it came through me from a higher intellect than mine.

The possibility of this is not my belief only. Every person proclaiming faith in God and Christ that I have known believe God communicates and guides them. It is an experience that many feel is real and steadfastly repeated. Isn't the connection with a POWER and LOVE greater than humankind's own a much proven TRUTH?

Index of Section Headings